CHILDHOOD AND ITS DISCONTENTS

CHILDHOOD AND ITS DISCONTENTS

The First Seamus Heaney Lectures

Edited by
Joseph Dunne *and* James Kelly

The Liffey Press
Dublin

Published by
The Liffey Press Ltd
Ashbrook House, 10 Main Street
Raheny, Dublin 5, Ireland
www.theliffeypress.com

A catalogue record of this book is
available from the British Library.

ISBN 1-904148-17-4

Cover painting: Walter Osborne, *A Boy Blowing Bubbles*,
Reproduced with the kind permission of The National Gallery of Ireland.

Printed in the Republic of Ireland by Colour Books Ltd.

CONTENTS

Preface .... *vii*

Notes on Contributors .... *ix*

Foreword by *Seamus Heaney* ....*xiii*

1: Introduction: Changing Perspectives on Childhoods 1
   Joseph Dunne and *James Kelly*

2: Birth of the Virtual Child: Origins of our Contradictory
   Images of Children 31
   John R. Gillis

3: The Cosmopolitan Family: Social Adaptation to a
   Changing World 51
   David Elkind

4: Suffer Little Children? The Historical Validity of Memoirs
   of Irish Childhood 69
   Diarmaid Ferriter

5: Too Much Knowledge, Too Much Fear: Curricular
   Developments in Irish Primary Schools 107
   Mark Morgan

6: Chaotic Girlhood: Narratives of Jewish Girl Survivors of
   Transnistria 123
   Ronit Lentin

7: The Concept of Childhood and the Experience of Children
    in Violently Divided Societies 159
        Marie Smyth

8: Education and Happiness 199
        Nel Noddings

PREFACE

Childhood requires little justification as a subject of enquiry, and the steady stream of work with this focus produced across several disciplines underlines its importance. Yet, there is much that remains unclear or that is contentious about the evolution of childhood and its present-day manifestations. 'Childhoods' was, for this reason, an appropriate theme for the inaugural Seamus Heaney Lectures that were held in St Patrick's College during the academic year 2000-01. The object of the series and, by extension, of this collection is to present a variety of perspectives on childhood from across a range of disciplines that will inform debate about its variegated and complex nature among educators, parents, policy makers, academics, students and the interested public.

It is a pleasant responsibility to acknowledge the advice and assistance of those individuals and interests that made both the lecture series and this publication a reality. We wish, in the first instance, to express particular thanks to Seamus Heaney who graciously agreed to allow his name to be associated with the lecture series and to write the Foreword to the collection. The task of inviting speakers and of organising the lecture series was shared among a committee of Academic Council, comprising Ciaran Sugrue, Pat Burke, Maura O'Connor, Eithne Kennedy, Marian Lyons and the editors. Especial acknowledgement is due Ciaran Sugrue, who acted as the committee's first convenor, and who played a key role in transforming a 'good idea' into reality, not least by generating funds that helped underwrite the cost of the series. The Committee has benefited greatly in this respect also from the support of the President of St Patrick's College, Dr Pauric Travers, whose personal commitment to the success of the series was emphasised by the support provided to the organising committee by his office. The contribution of Ms Theresa O'Farrell deserves particular acknowledgement.

The Committee wishes also to express its gratitude to Professor Mary Daly, Dr Ann Looney, Professor Patrick Crotty, Mr Martin French, Mr Martin Ward, Mr Paul Murphy, Ms Aine Carroll and, of course, to the audiences that contributed by their presence and by their observations to making each of the lectures an occasion as well as an educational experience. The preparation of the lectures for publication has been assisted greatly by a generous grant-in-aid of publication from the Research Committee of St Patrick's College.

Finally, it is a pleasure formally to thank the seven speakers whose addresses printed in these pages served both to stimulate and to provoke, and our colleagues on the organising committee for their good counsel and support.

Joseph Dunne and James Kelly
September 2002

NOTES ON CONTRIBUTORS

Joseph Dunne teaches Philosophy and co-ordinates the Human Development programme in the Education Department at St Patrick's College. He is the author of *Back to the Rough Ground: 'Phronesis' and 'Techne' in Modern Philosophy and in Aristotle* (1993, 1997) and editor (with Attracta Ingram and Frank Litton) of *Questioning Ireland: Debates in Political Philosophy and Public Policy* (2000).

David Elkind is Professor of Child Development at Tufts University, Massachusetts. He is the author of many books including *Images of the Young Child* (1993), *Ties that Stress: The New Family Imbalance* (1994), and *Reinventing Childhood: Raising and Educating Children in a Changing World* (1998). He is currently working on a book tentatively titled *Leadership Parenting: Meeting the Childrearing Challenges of the Postmodern World*.

Diarmaid Ferriter is a lecturer in the History Department, St Patrick's College. He is the author of *A Nation of Extremes: The Pioneers in Twentieth-century Ireland* (1999), *Local Government in Twentieth-century Ireland* (2001) and (with Colm Tóibín) *The Irish Famine: A Documentary* (2001). He is currently working on a social history of twentieth-century Ireland.

John R. Gillis is Professor of History at Rutgers University and the author, among other works, of *Youth and History: Tradition and Change in European Age Relations from 1750 to the Present* (1974), *For*

Better or Worse: British Marriages, 1600 to the Present (1985, 1988) and *A World of Their Own Making: Myth, Ritual and the Quest for Family Values*, which was published by Harvard University Press in 1996. He is currently engaged on a geo-historical study of Atlantic islands centring on their role in the formation of the Atlantic world.

James Kelly is Head of the History Department, St Patrick's College. Among other works, he is the author of *Henry Flood: Patriots and Politics in Eighteenth-century Ireland* (1998) and *Gallows Speeches from Eighteenth-century Ireland* (2001).

Ronit Lentin is Director of the M.Phil. in Ethnic and Racial Studies and a lecturer in the Department of Sociology at Trinity College, Dublin. Among other works, she is the editor of *Gender and Catastrophe* (1997) and *The Expanding Nation: Towards a Multi-ethnic Ireland* (1999), and the author of *Israel and the Daughters of the Shoah: Re-occupying the Territories of Silence* (2000). She is also a novelist; her most recent is *Songs on the Death of Children* (1996).

Mark Morgan is Head of the Education Department, St Patrick's College. He is the author of many reports on aspects of the modern Irish educational system and on substance abuse, including (with Joel Grube) *Drinking among Post-primary School Pupils* (1994), *Report to the Minister for Education on the International Adult Literacy Survey* (1997) and *Drug Use Prevention: An Overview of Research* (2001).

Nel Noddings is Professor of Philosophy and Education at Teachers College, Columbia University, and Lee L. Jacks Professor of Child Education Emerita at Stanford University. She is the author of, among other works, *Caring: A Feminine Approach to Ethics and Moral Education* (1984) and *Starting from Home: Care and Social Policy* (2002).

Marie Smyth, a Jennings Randolph Senior Fellow at the United States Institute of Peace in Washington DC for 2002–3, is Chief Executive of the Institute for Conflict Research, Belfast, and a member of staff of the University of Ulster. She is the author of, among other works, *Half the Battle: Understanding the Impact of the Troubles on Children and Young People* (1998); (with M. Scott) *The Youth Quest 2000 Survey: Young People's Experiences and View of Life in Northern Ireland* (2000); (with Mike Morrissey) *Northern Ireland after the Good Friday Agreement: Victims, Grievance and Blame* (2002); and (with Gillian Robinson) *Researching Violently Divided Societies: Ethical and Methodological Issues* (2001). She has edited (with M.T. Fay) *Personal Accounts from Northern Ireland's Troubles* (2000), and other works.

FOREWORD

Seamus Heaney

A lecture series named in one's honour? When I got the letter of proposal from the President of St Patrick's College, I was uneasy. Valuable as the series was going to be, was there not something questionable about allowing oneself to be elevated by it, through mere association? But when I recollected my years of association with colleges of education, first in the English Department of St Joseph's in Belfast and then in Carysfort College, I thought again. I remembered the problem and the effort of devising courses and lecture topics which would (ideally) fulfil two aims: on the one hand, help to prepare the students for their life as professionals in the classroom and, on the other, contribute to the students' development as cultured and confident individuals. And since the proposed lectures were concerned with this same need to integrate the practical and the speculative side of the educator's work, I thought, well, yes, OK.

The contributions to the book do indeed exhibit an admirable spread of interest. They range from an interrogation of the new curriculum in Irish schools — a chapter to which policy makers should pay close attention — to more philosophical and historical enquiries into the construction of childhood and the child as subjects in themselves. There are different and complementary satisfactions available here, for both the specialist and the interested general reader. The graphs and tables, for example, in Marie Smyth's account of childhood in divided societies such as Northern Ireland and South Africa, are immediately fascinating (my own eye tends to glide over facts and figures marshalled in this way, but here the statistics and their interpretation gave me pause); and the challenge which Diarmaid Ferriter sets out at the conclusion of his chapter — to fit the literary genre of the memoir, so favoured by Irish writers, into a framework of historical research — is one that is bound to stimulate readers as well as researchers.

*   *   *

Often as I went through these pages I thought of William Wordsworth, the poet who had such an original and epoch-making interest not just in the growth of his own mind but in many of the general questions still being raised in these lectures. Questions of happiness, such as those that concern Nel Noddings: how can the human creature be fitted for life in the modern world? Questions of adaptation: how do our traditional ideas and our moral being square with new social conditions which keep arriving at ever greater speed (a question that David Elkind explores, for example, in Chapter 3)? Questions about one's answerability to or for human suffering.

Just over 200 years ago, Wordsworth formulated the notion that the experience of beauty and fear in early childhood had a formative and positive effect on the adult person's capacities and disposition. It was a poet's conception, arrived at by somebody who had not only lived through intense happiness and unhappiness in his early days, but possessed also a sophisticated grasp of contemporary psychological theories about consciousness and identity. And as a conception, it has proved remarkably durable.

Wordsworth's autobiographical poem, 'The Prelude' (1805), is one of the most important documents in the history of what Professor Gillis calls (in Chapter 2) the virtual child. When he made an inquisition of himself in his late twenties, Wordsworth remembered how the emotional sympathies of the pre-pubertal boy had been enlarged by living in unmediated relationship with the cloudscapes and mountainsides and lake surfaces of Cumberland. Equally he remembered that the country people he dwelt among showed no signs of either personal affectation or class distinction, and realised that this rural society had convinced him of the natural dignity and equality of human beings. And he was convinced also that his moral sense had been fostered and confirmed by what we would now call the projection of his guilt feelings upon the landscape: when, for example, he stole out on a rowing expedition in another person's boat, the overshadowing cliff seemed to stalk him in a minatory fashion, as if it were some huge conscience enforcer coming after him across the water.

Reading the lectures — so different in their emphases, so varied in methodology, so reflective of the sensibility and the discrimination of the person who delivered them — I am struck by the continuing usefulness of the Wordsworthian paradigm. A century before Freud (whose name, strangely, is little mentioned in the course of these discussions), Wordsworth announced that the child was father to the man. Although he did not name it, he had in fact located the unconscious as a powerful determining factor in the individual's sense of identity and purpose and — to use the cheerful and efficient term Nel Noddings introduces in Chapter 8 — Subjective Well Being.

Wordsworth lived, however, before the Holocaust and the atomic bomb. For him and his contemporaries, the word 'fear' had the aura of primal experience about it; his was not the insuperable fear that the Jewish children in Transnistria (about whom Ronit Lentin writes so powerfully in Chapter 6) were exposed to. Wordsworthian 'fear' pointed to the reality of an unknown and scaresome dimension beyond us, but it also suggested that as human beings we were still fit to bear this reality, were even braced by it and certainly the better for facing it. And a hundred years later, in a poem of Robert Frost's entitled 'The Fear' — about a woman's sixth-sensing of an intruder near her house at night in the country — that same understanding of the human subject as 'an inmate of this active universe' still persisted. Indeed, the old idea that there is a match between consciousness and the conditions it has to survive is explicitly endorsed by the Frost poem. In the woman's dialogue with the speaker in the dark, a voice which seems to carry the weight of the poet's approval tells her (and the reader), 'Every child should have the memory/Of at least one long-after-bedtime walk'.

Such confidence in the possibility of achieving a balance between the rational and the irrational factors within ourselves, in our ability to negotiate the desirable and inexorable elements in the historical reality we inhabit, becomes harder and harder to maintain. In a world where the cultures of shame and *civilité* alluded to by Marie Smyth no longer regulate behaviour, a world where (to quote Wordsworth one last time) 'a multitude of causes, unknown to former times, are now acting with combined force to . . . reduce [the mind] to a state of almost savage torpor', in such a world educators are forced to consider with renewed urgency their purposes and their methods. These lectures constitute a vigorous and timely contribution to that work of self-interrogation and goal-setting.

Chapter 1

INTRODUCTION: CHANGING PERSPECTIVES ON CHILDHOODS

Joseph Dunne **and** *James Kelly*

I

Never have children and their lives attracted so much attention or elicited such concern as in recent years in the liberal democratic societies of the industrialised world. With unprecedented awareness of the dignity and value of childhood now widely shared, children are seen as unique sources of hope and the proper subjects of special cherishing and care. This valorising of childhood is accompanied, however, by an increasing awareness of the dangers and pitfalls that now threaten children. Childhood, we have been forced to recognise, is subject to conflicting pressures and stirs up much ambivalence and uncertainty.

There is, on the one hand, more sensitivity to children's needs but, on the other, a sense of depleting resources within families and communities to meet them. What we call 'childhood' is the product of an increasing tendency to segregate and shelter the young. But this tendency, afoot in the West over many centuries, seems now to be reversing in the face of indiscriminate accessibility of new media and the targeting of children as consumers by

increasingly unfettered markets. A child-centred rhetoric prevails
in primary schools; but the wider socio-economic matrix in which
these schools are inserted — and especially the organisation of
work — is increasingly less child-friendly. While childhood is ex-
tolled as a privileged phase of the human lifespan — a care-free
time to be enjoyed for its own sake — children are regarded with
growing anxiety as the nation's greatest resource for the future, on
no account to be allowed to run free. Louder calls for them to 'live
their childhood fully' are met by the obstinate reality that there
are now fewer spaces where they can do so safely. There is much
cultural advance in the direction of children's emancipation — the
extension and vindication of their rights, greater acknowledgement of their autonomy, and growing access on their part to
knowledge and power — but this is accompanied by much
greater concern for their protection, manifest for example in pressures to increase the ages of criminal responsibility, compulsory
school attendance, and entry to the workforce. There is greater
awareness than ever of the extent to which children have been
abused and victimised, in supposed settings of 'care' in the advanced industrial societies as well as on the streets and in sweat-
shops of the 'third world'; but this awareness finds a counterpoint
in shocked incomprehension at the horrors that children themselves can perpetrate, as revealed for example by the Jamie Bulger
case in Britain or numerous well-publicised killings by minors in
the US.

In the Republic of Ireland, this intensification of interest in
childhood is reflected in the number of state initiatives directed
towards children over the past decade. We have seen the ratifica-
tion of the United Nations Convention on the Rights of the Child,
a new Childcare Act, the creation of a ministry of state with responsibility for children, and the enactment of a Children's Bill.
More ambitiously, there was the launching of a National Children's Strategy, 'Our Children, Their Lives', which recognises, in
a manner scarcely conceivable less than a generation ago, children's entitlement to a 'voice' in all matters affecting them — and
which, accordingly, proposes the establishment of an Ombuds-

man for Children as well as a Children's Parliament (or *Dáil na nÓg*). As part of this strategy, there is a new commitment to facilitate and to fund research so that 'children's lives may be better understood'; towards this end, a major national longitudinal study of Irish children's wellbeing is now underway. These initiatives are in addition to a raft of educational measures, such as the publication of a white paper on early childhood education, a major revision of the primary school curriculum, a comprehensive Education Act, and special provisions for schools in areas of disadvantage that have been included in several 'National Agreements' between the government and the 'social partners'. And all of this legislation and policy development, constituting an explicitly reforming agenda, has taken place against the backdrop of increasing awareness — in response to a succession of often harrowing revelations and exposures — of the extent to which children in Ireland have been exploited and abused within the home, in extra-familial institutions, and in other settings where they have been prey to adults in whom they might most have been expected to repose their trust.

II

The greatly enlarged profile of children in popular consciousness and in state activity has found a counterpart in a new level of academic engagement with childhood as the site of issues that are as vexing and contested as they are important. Two distinct though related features of this most recent scholarly work, amounting to what might be termed 'paradigm shifts' in the area, deserve special mention. First, there is a growing sense that much earlier research was limited because it was conducted *on* children rather than *with* them. Its methodological frame emphasised the purported neutrality and detachment of the researcher, the isolation and control of the data to be investigated — various aspects of the observable behaviour or experience of children — and replicable, generalisable results which could be taken as universally valid. From the perspective of a more recent kind of research, however, this methodological frame, for all its putative rigour, yields only a partial and impoverished view of children's real capabilities and actual lives. It needs to be complemented by other approaches better attuned to the 'life-worlds' of children, more resourceful in catching the texture and nuance of their speech, action, thought and feeling as embedded in contexts that are immediately mean- ingful to themselves even if not readily amenable to the objective categorisation and measurement of accredited science. In these other approaches — more naturalistic, ethnographic and ex- pressly interactive — children's 'voice' and 'agency' come more into relief. No longer comparable to the 'mute' subject-groups of traditional anthropology, they are seen to have distinctive inten- tions, projects and sense-making capacities that can be better un- derstood by more hermeneutically sensitive (and therefore more adequately reflective and self-critical) adult researchers.

The second distinctive feature of recent research on childhood is its multi-disciplinary range. For most of the twentieth century, children and childhood were seen as the almost exclusive pre- serve of psychology. Or, rather, psychology seemed to be alone among the social sciences in recognising them as worthy objects of close study — consider the profile of developmental psychology and in particular Piaget's important work on the evolution of cognitive capacities in children, or the seminal influence of Freud's psychoanalytic explorations, with their emphasis on childhood as the crucially determinative chapter of the life-story, the uniquely significant source, for weal or woe, of human charac- ter. The extension of the study of childhood beyond psychology to other disciplines has arisen in the context of a critique of the 'naturalism' of both developmental psychology and psychoanaly- sis — the assumption, that is to say, that there are, first, fixed and invariant stages of development (e.g. of intellectual competence or emotional responsiveness) and, second, ineluctable drives and psychic mechanisms, both of which are to be taken as trans- cultural 'givens' of the human species, available to context- neutral, scientific investigation. And this critique within psychol- ogy has been bolstered by the emergence of complementary critical impulses in disciplines such as history and sociology. In history, for example, the traditional concern with power, and the consequent emphasis on military, political and diplomatic affairs, has been diluted by engagement with the everyday lives of 'ordinary' people, especially women and children. Within the wider context of a new flourishing of cultural history, children's lives and the forces that have shaped them have become an important subject for research.

As a result of this work, and the emergence of a new sociology of childhood significantly influenced by it, scholarly attention to children now locates them more firmly within specific social, cultural, and political contexts. In a way analogous to the opening up of gender as a *topos* across many disciplines a few decades ago — with a new focus on female and male identities as not just subject to biological imperatives but as shaped by social and cultural processes as well as by changes in material conditions — childhood is now seen less as a natural phase than as a socio-historical construct. Much that is imputed to 'childhood' as a universal phenomenon turns out, on closer analysis, to be the product of a specific culture or historical epoch. 'The child' as a construct gives way to the rich particularity of children with different backgrounds, needs, interests and constraints. Normative claims for any single version of 'childhood' become enormously problematic when exposed to the full range of *childhoods* that cultural and historical study now brings to our attention. Not that we must forego any judgements as to what constitutes proper flourishing for children; rather, critically grounding these judgements involves unpacking and perhaps dispensing with prized elements of our all too easy assumptions about what gives substance and value to 'childhood'.

The essays in this book, composed for oral delivery to a non-specialist audience, offer a sample of the kind of scholarly work now directed to children and childhood. They reflect much more, it should be said, the second rather the first of the two shifts just adverted to: though not entirely absent, transcripts, or close-textured analysis of children's lives in which their own voices and

idioms claim a significant place, do not feature here. But a
strongly multi-disciplinary focus is evident throughout the volume. While two of the contributions are by psychologists (Elkind
and Morgan), it is significant that both are concerned to interpret
and evaluate the impact of broad social changes on the lives of
children. There are essays, too, from historians (Gillis and Ferriter), one tracing the genealogy of 'childhood' as a potent image
for western adults, and the other reconstructing the lives of children of different religious, geographical and class backgrounds
from a wide range of memoirs and autobiographical writings by
Irish men and women over the past several decades. Two other
essays are by sociologists (Smyth and Lentin), both devoted to
understanding the lot of children in two quite different troubled
societies, Northern Ireland during years of civil strife, and Transnistria during the worst excesses of the Second World War. Finally, there is an essay by a philosopher (Noddings) which, with
particular reference to children and the kind of education that
they now receive, reflects on a central and abiding question for
human beings: the meaning and content of happiness and
whether, or by what means, it is to be attained.

III

If childhood is socially constructed it is mainly of course a construct of *adults*. This is true in the obvious sense that it is adults
who give birth to children, create the environments in which their
lives take shape, and largely determine the kinds of knowledge
and experience that their childhoods will be devoted to acquiring.
To acknowledge this is to see childhood not as a state in itself but
as constituted through its relationship with adulthood. However,
this relationship also has a converse side: in ways that are less obvious and less easy to acknowledge, adulthood is constituted
through its relation to childhood. The significance that childhood
assumes, then, may say less about real children than about the
adults whose symbolic investments and emotional projections
they carry. It is this side of the relationship between children and

adults, and its complex elaboration in modern western history, that John Gillis analyses in the opening essay of the collection. The contemporary fascination with children, evidenced in the extent to which they are photographed or in the strength of the secular rituals now centred on them (e.g. christening as a celebration of their birth itself — and not of their reception into a community of faith — or birthdays as symbolic markers of their progress through childhood, or Christmas as a sentimentalised occasion for benevolence towards them) is, as Gillis points out, a relatively new phenomenon. Before the rise of what he calls the 'virtual child', a creature of adult imagination which has become a master symbol of our culture, children received little symbolic regard and death, not birth, was held to be the crucial personal moment.

Gillis relates the rise of the virtual child to several displacements of sensibility experienced most acutely by the advanced Protestant middle classes in the nineteenth century. A crisis of religious faith coincided with a profound transformation of the basis of family life brought about by the Industrial Revolution. As the household ceded its economic functions to factory and office, the older family, based on real relations within the domestic economy and inclusive of non-kin, contracted to the biologically constituted nuclear family, with the father assuming the role of breadwinner (and, increasingly, emotional absentee) and the woman assuming an all-consuming identity as mother within a domestic sphere increasingly devoid of a productive function. It was within this new kind of family constellation, with children fewer in number and more emotionally irreplaceable within each unit, that childhood came to be endowed with a new, almost sacred, significance. A secularised adult imagination transposed the Christian tropes of fall and redemption from the religious to the familial arenas. Paradise lost became childhood lost as, identified with innocence and unsullied simplicity, childhood became a focus of intense nostalgia — especially for adult males expelled from the newly feminised world to which children were now seen to belong. This intensification of sentiment around children arose at a time, so Gillis suggests, when imperial conquest had ex-

hausted the inhabited Earth's potential to yield places onto which
the advanced European mind could project images of an uncorrupted nature now deemed to be irretrievably forfeit to its own
industrial drive.

The discovery of 'that mythic country called childhood' was
thus a response to adult dislocation and adult need. With the crisis of faith and transformation of family that shadowed industrial
and imperial endeavour, childhood became a new reference point.
As a 'myth of both origins and destiny', it symbolised a gifted and
blissful state once enjoyed and perhaps sometime to be recovered
— if only through the kind of imaginative recollection that became such a prominent feature in the new vogue for memoir and
autobiography or, later, in the work of recuperation and reconstruction that was to become the heart of psychotherapy.
Throughout his essay Gillis is alive to the gap between imagined
childhood and real children. Not only may the latter's lives be
limited by intransigent pressures in the real world, they may be
damaged by the myth itself — as indeed, also, may the lives of
adults. For the splitting involved in any strong idealisation creates
an unassimilated 'other': with the angel there is always the demon
or the monster — in this case, the 'bad' or unconforming child
who is treated all the more uncomprehendingly the more adults
are in thrall to the ideal image. But in fact this split between
'good' and 'bad' children is only a refraction of the more basic
split that also needs vigilant interrogation: that between adults
and children. For this latter split may easily serve to obscure not
only an aspect of children's potential — for rational thought and
effective action — but also an aspect of adults' potential — for
wonder, playfulness and intense, non-instrumental absorption. It
may, that is to say, compromise the possibilities of a more integral
humanity for *both* children and adults.

If John Gillis depicts the cult of childhood as an outgrowth of
high modernity with its canonisation of the nuclear family, it is
the demise of this family-type as cultural norm in the transition to
'post-modernity' that David Elkind analyses in Chapter 3. In the
post-industrial society that we now inhabit, the nuclear family

seems to have become maladaptive, increasingly to be replaced by what Elkind calls the 'cosmopolitan family'. Whereas the nuclear family reflected the conservative values and clearly demarcated roles of the industrial age, the cosmopolitan family accommodates the value-relativity, flexible role-definitions and fluid identities of the information society. More open and plural in its structure — so that it embraces single-parent families (unmarried or divorced), families of two parents (married or cohabiting) where both work outside the home, families (with or without children) where one or both partners have been in previous relationships, and families where both partners/parents are of the same sex — the cosmopolitan family implies a new conception of parent and of child. Whereas in the case of the nuclear family the fact of biological parenthood was taken to endow a couple with a natural parental authority — or to trigger an inbuilt disposition towards wise childcare — the cosmopolitan family accommodates more easily the fact of parental ineptitude (iconised by Homer Simpson).

Like Gillis, Elkind locates parenting against a wider societal backdrop; in this case, the information society requires the release of women into the workforce and hence an acceptance of the kind of extra-familial care that was frowned on in the heyday of the nuclear family. Elkind sees this as related, in turn, to a different conception of childhood. Innocence has receded as the emblematical quality, while the traditional culture of childhood — embodied in games, pastimes, rhymes, songs and riddles, transmitted informally without adult mediation in playgrounds and on the streets — has retreated as public spaces have become more opaque to children and a sense of safety is eroded by changes in transport and more widespread fears of violence. Children's lives have become more scripted and scheduled, more subject to adult surveillance, while their culture is now the largely fabricated one mediated by the consumer market — the world of Pokemon, Nintendo, Power Rangers and Playstation.

Elkind's overall theoretical perspective is that of a kind of social evolutionism: he perceives the family, and with it the roles of parents and children, as a subsystem that must willy-nilly establish equilibrium with the wider social system of which it is part. From this perspective it is simply a fact that the cosmopolitan family accommodates better the realities of post-modern society, if only because its own very instability — in terms of flexibility, mobility, and capacity for self-reinvention — is better adapted to the instability of the wider society. Though clearly drawn to the value-neutrality that goes with this perspective (and is so generally prized by established social science), Elkind does not eschew value judgments. Or rather he does not fail to raise the crucial question of whether, even if the cosmopolitan family is more fitted for survival in contemporary advanced societies, cosmopolitan childhood is still a satisfactory state for children.

Elkind's answer to this question, though nuanced, is in the end quite definite. He sees *competence* replacing innocence as the most defining feature of childhood. And he recognises positive aspects to the new demands for, and possibilities of, competence on the part of children. The kind of capability required to negotiate settings of non-parental care even at a very young age is, he believes, to be welcomed (though this is by no means to endorse the quality of many such extra-familial settings or the degree of state support they receive). Likewise, he sees positive gains in children's adeptness with the new information and communication technologies where they often markedly surpass their elders and where children with specific disabilities — hearing or sight impairment, for example — are particular beneficiaries. However, he also sees a downside to the postulation of child competence. While children are assumed to be media- and market-savvy, for example, he does not believe that, faced with endless information and limitless options, they are competent to make the necessary discriminations and choices. And his final overall judgement is that while the cosmopolitan family is more responsive to the needs of *parents*, children's needs were better served by the *nuclear* family. (His reasons for this conclusion stem from a basic intuition that, being immature in ways that too easily come against them, children have 'a continuing need for adult guidance and moral leadership' — a need denied when '[u]nfortunately the cosmopolitan egalitarian ethos was inappropriately extended' to them and when, as in post-modern conditions, clear societal markers of the attainment of specific stages along a developmental path have been abandoned.)

IV

Elkind's conclusion — that in the newly emergent kind of society (of which the United States is the most advanced example) adult advantage is purchased at the price of child disadvantage — if true, surely raises the gravest questions. However, if one is tempted to suppose that this conclusion vindicates or justifies efforts to restore the kind of culture that obtained in Ireland for most of the twentieth century, the essay by Diarmaid Ferriter may do much to give one pause. Ferriter shows how the kind of idealisation of childhood identified by Gillis was embraced in nationalist rhetoric in Ireland from the early part of the twentieth century: the nation to be reclaimed from colonial conquest and childhood shared the same imputation of untarnished innocence and goodness. It is the gulf between this rhetoric and the reality of the life experiences of many Irish children that is Ferriter's primary focus. His means of accessing this '"underbelly" of Irish state and society at a crucial time in the development of modern Ireland' is through memoirs and autobiographical writings. In ironic contrast to de Valera's famous evocation of the 'romping of sturdy children' around 'cosy homesteads', Ferriter finds 'few children romping sturdily in the books under consideration here'. To be sure, there are depictions of stable and happy childhoods and indeed of some idyllic ones. Still, a picture emerges of much 'calculated savagery' towards children within families, routine beatings in schools, and cruelty and abuse in reformatories and industrial schools (institutions maintained in Ireland well after their abandonment in Britain and never open to proper public scrutiny). The themes that emerge strongly in Ferriter's reconstruction from his selected texts are the gendered nature of the mistreatment of children (fathers emerge very badly indeed — 'no mouse was ever more wary of the cat than we were of our father' — while the picture of mothers is altogether more sympathetic), the powerfully pervasive influence of class (not least in determining the quality of access to health services and education), and the ambiguous role of religion (often a source of comfort but also of intimidation and resentment).

Some important methodological questions arise about Ferriter's undertaking. Does such autobiographical writing, even if his is a representative sample, truly represent children's lives in twentieth-century Ireland (or does *negative* experience inevitably exert a greater pressure towards cathartic expression)? Given that all this writing is by *adults* recalling their childhoods, how reliably can a child's actual experience be rendered in subsequent recollection by his or her later self? And what kinds of critical restraints and contextual accommodations may be required in judging the conduct of an earlier society from the vantage point — including, not least the changed material conditions — of a later society? While Ferriter is aware of these questions, it is not his task here to answer them — nor does he prejudge what the force of properly balanced answers may be. The main methodological claim that he does make seems both modest and warranted: that the kind of texts he has examined, narrating first-person experience, deserve to be taken into account, in addition and as a complement to official public records, if 'meaningful and critical histories of modern Ireland are to be written' — histories that will deconstruct well-sponsored myths and enable us to understand better not only 'what happened' but 'what it felt like'. It might be added, perhaps, that if the history of childhood is to be adequately written in the future there will be need, too, for a kind of data that still hardly exists (though research under the rubric of the first paradigm shift noted above now recognises its significance): testimonies, in whatever form, giving voice to children themselves.

Since Ferriter's enquiry here is pioneering, it is impossible to say what the longer view of the import of his targeted genre of writing will be. But, from his analysis, it is at least 'strongly tempting' to conclude that 'the greatest blot on twentieth-century

Irish society's copybook was its treatment of children'. It must be acknowledged at the same time that in the final decades of that century significant efforts (adverted to earlier) were made to lighten the burden on children and to enhance the quality of their lives. In the essay that follows Ferriter's, which focuses specifically on school experience, Mark Morgan identifies some of these advances. Whereas in the 1960s 'early school leaving' referred to the 20 per cent of children who did not complete even primary schooling, its connotation has since shifted a full level — it is the failure to complete *secondary* education by significantly less than twenty percent of the relevant age-cohort that it now marks. Or, to take another example, since the introduction of the 'new curriculum' in 1971, and especially since the abolition of corporal punishment in 1984, children seem to *enjoy* school in a manner perhaps inconceivable to those memoirists of an earlier generation who feature in Ferriter's essay (the publication and reception of some of these memoirs in recent years, and the public ventilation of their pain, is itself partly attributable to a new climate).

Such welcome improvements apart, Morgan's perspective on recent educational developments is critical rather than celebratory. He argues that attempts at curricular reform in the primary school have been vitiated by the inclusion of too many subjects and by a correlative failure to identify what should be central or core (the 1971 curriculum doubled the number of subjects while the 1999 revision mandated a significant further increase). He points to dismaying evidence that this relentless addition of content has been accompanied by a diminution in children's acquisition of 'higher order cognitive skills' and a consequent decline in their ability to deploy knowledge appropriately and resourcefully in out-of-school settings as well as by the stubborn persistence of the same level of basic literacy problems in young teenagers as existed in the 1970s.

As well as offering a general critique of curricular overload, Morgan has a more specific target: the tendency to make the school curriculum directly responsive to societal concerns, so that the identification of a particular social problem or dysfunction is

immediately translated into a curricular package (if not entire
subject) whose in-school consumption by pupils is intended to
address it. He argues that such well-intentioned efforts — directed at problems such as substance abuse, crime, or suicide —
are not only ineffective but counter-productive: by amplifying attention to them, they *increase* children's propensity to engage in
the very problem-behaviours that they are intended to combat.
On his analysis, the most effective antidote to self-destructive or
anti-social behaviours is not information about or even opportunities to discuss them but rather tackling their underlying causes.
But this analysis does nothing to diminish the role of schools in
coping with various social ills. For school failure *is itself* one of the
main underlying causes of recourse to drug-taking and criminality. Conversely, the acquisition of basic skills, and in particular an
ability and disposition to read, is highly correlated with construc-
tive engagement in, for example, communal and (perhaps surprisingly) sporting activity. Much 'busyness' with socially informed
curricula, Morgan suggests (here echoing Gillis), is an expression
of adult fear rather than a rational response to problems or an effective help to children in dealing with them. Nor are children
well served when, out of concern for their safety or self-esteem,
adults would protect them from experiences of failure, frustration
or disappointment. To the contrary, it is only in being motivated
to take on challenges, where they deal with rather than avoid the
real possibility of failure, that children can develop competence —
the essential quality (also emphasised by Elkind) that Morgan sees
as the cause rather than the consequence of the now much
vaunted 'self-esteem'.

It is a clear implication of Morgan's argument that teachers
should stick to their lasts — that schools should concentrate on
their properly educational function and not be made to chase after
every new item on the agenda of social concern. This is surely an
important position to take in debate about the nature and role of
education. In such fundamental debate (whose very absence from
the policy scene is a matter of great concern), two interesting
questions that arise from this position — though they lie beyond

the scope of Morgan's present essay — will perhaps be worth pursuing. Even if educational failure, defined as the non-attainment of basic skills, can be seen as a cause of many social ills, to what extent is it itself *also* an *effect* of *other* causes, and how much leverage on these other causes — socio-economic in nature and centrally related to poverty and inequality — can schools be realistically expected to exert? And — a crucial question with respect to childhood as well as to education — can 'basic' or 'core' skills be defined in such a way that they not only involve more than rote drill but also do not exclude (as 'non-basic' or 'peripheral') areas of the arts such as music, drama, painting, and dance that have long been curricular cinderellas?

V

If the last few decades have seen conspicuous efforts at educational reform in the Republic of Ireland, in Northern Ireland they have been a time of great civil strife whose impact on children is the subject of Marie Smyth's contribution. Smyth provides copious quantitative documentation of the extent to which children have suffered or witnessed (or in some cases caused) death or injury or have been damaged in their lives through the death or injury of parents or siblings, the experience of intimidation, bullying or punishment beatings, or the disruption of their lives in the home, school or peer group. She also correlates the incidence of such experiences with differences in age, gender, geographical location, and religious and political affiliation. And she complements these research findings with excerpts from oral testimony by a 15-year-old girl in Northern Ireland and semi-autobiographical writing by a young male from South Africa (a society which she parallels with Northern Ireland). In vivid and searing detail, unmediated by any interpretative apparatus or political agenda, these excerpts give voice, in the one case, to a girl's exposure to murder and mayhem within her own home, with no hint of restraint by the killer in the presence of children and little ability on the part of traumatised parent figures to provide protec-

tion or relief; and, in the other, to a boy's experience of rape, prostitution, violence and drugs.

Smyth's purpose is not just to profile the terrible experiences
of some children in Northern Ireland (and localisation of the conflict, she stresses, has tended to confine them to a few areas,
mostly ones of economic and social disadvantage) but to ask
whether, in the face of such extremity, 'childhood' can be sal-
vaged as a concept applicable to these young people. Following
the influential work of the French cultural historian, Philippe
Ariès, she sees childhood as a specific achievement of cultural
evolution in the West involving, from the Renaissance onwards,
the gradual segregation of children from the adult world, a recognition of their vulnerability and special neediness, and a corresponding acceptance of adult responsibility to care for them. This
responsibility was exercised within a family environment increasingly concerned for privacy and moral uplift and later augmented
by the modern state's assumption of a protective role through
watchdog legislation and the granting of entitlements to public
education and welfare. More specifically, however, Smyth follows
the American educational theorist Neil Postman (himself influenced by Ariès and the historical sociologist, Norbert Elias) in seeing *shame* as a crucial element in the cultural construction of
childhood. Shame is involved in recognising some aspects of human experience — especially those related to sex and death — as
charged with a significance that, among other things, requires
their occlusion from children (some cultural secrets are good);
and, relatedly, it powers a concern for various forms of contextu-
ally appropriate decorum and restraint. Shame can be seen as
constitutive of childhood in two ways: first, the extended period
in which young people have to learn to internalise it *is* their childhood; and, second, without its pervasive, unobtrusive presence in
a culture, adults are incapable of establishing the conditions in
which 'childhood' can exist let alone flourish.

From Smyth's perspective, it is most deeply through depleting
what might be called the 'shame capital' of a society that violent
division impacts on childhood. As she sees it, this happens very

crucially through a transformation of personal life whereby group identity (a life-or-death determinant in some circumstances) tends to trump individuation, while private feeling, in terms of grief, fear or despair, is either transmuted into stoic indifference or re-routed through the publicly dominant register of anger and griev-ance. This cauterisation and distortion of feeling fits with a vic-timhood that can be claimed by both sides to a conflict, acting to legitimate further violence that can be blamed on the original per-petrator. Inter-communal violence tends to weaken the power of shame by diminishing a sense of responsibility and inducing an absolutist identification and black-and-white thinking in each be-leaguered side (*in extremis*, complexity is 'a luxury indulged in by those who are safe'). It thus creates conditions in which adulthood is a more difficult achievement and, in which — for this very rea-son — childhood is a more precarious state. Here 'adulthood' and 'childhood' are normative categories very clearly demarcated from each other (adulthood is 'a social, moral and intellectual state dif-ferentiated from the state of childhood') *and* altogether interde-pendent (enjoying a childhood is a prerequisite for becoming properly adult, while securely established adulthood creates the conditions in which childhood can exist and be enjoyed).

To whatever degree this analysis may be applicable in the case of Northern Ireland, a breach in such a clear boundary between childhood and adulthood is already identifiable in the groups who have conduced the armed conflict there. Both republican and loyalist paramilitaries, as well as the British army, have recruited and armed persons under 18 (the age under which one is recog-nised by the United Nations Convention as being still a child), and among the many melancholy statistics given by Smyth are the numbers of under-age fatalities from each group. Despite the dismay occasioned by this fact, however, there may still be a diffi-cult issue to be faced about the line of demarcation between chil-dren and adults — about where, or how clearly and firmly, it should be drawn. This issue seems unavoidable if one accepts the force of Gillis's exposure of the limiting effects — on both children and adults — of an over-determined emphasis on the *differences*

between them. Moreover, it may reveal a deep and as yet unre-
solved tension in our most advanced and enlightened attitudes
towards childhood — reflecting indeed parallel tensions with respect to gender, ethnicity, disability and, more generally, the politics of multiculturalism: how, in negotiating ineliminable dualities
in all such spheres, to give due weight to the universal and the
particular, to what is common and what is distinctive. At one
point in her essay, referring to the contrast between provisions
concerning children in the new constitution of South Africa and
the lack of any formal recognition of their role in the conflict in
Northern Ireland, Smyth writes: 'This is at once a hopeful and depressing augury — hopeful in that perhaps it signals some residual shame at children's involvement, depressing in that it may
rather be a sign of the general low status of children in the wider
society [of Northern Ireland].' This remark may reflect a quite
general ambivalence about claims for children's *empowerment* and
agency (as a right to be held in common with adults) *and* claims
for their *protection* and care (as a right distinctive to them). It is a
still largely unacknowledged ambivalence that we in the Republic
may have to confront if our recently published National Children's Strategy ever moves beyond aspirational rhetoric to real
implementation.

Smyth's understanding of the mutual implication between
childhood and adulthood leaves her with a poignant formulation
of the task facing a society troubled for more than a generation by
war and strife: how to help some people who have never had a
childhood to become adults — or how to find ways of 'compensating for lost childhoods, in order to prevent further such losses'.
For those faced with this task there is not much comfort in Ronit
Lentin's reflection on 'ruptured childhood' in a very different cultural and political setting — the transitory enclave of Transnistria
in the southern Ukraine, which was created as a Nazi gift to Romania, and to where that country transported most of its Jewish
population between 1941 and 1943. Like Ferriter and Smyth, Lentin works from first-person testimonies — in her case, those of
women who survived, as girls, the horrors of these mass transpor-

tations (and the terrible pogroms that preceded it). But, unlike the other two essayists, Lentin gives thematic attention to the role of language and silence, and in particular to the complicated dynamics and blockages of *memory*, in dealing with deeply traumatising events in childhood. Moreover, as the daughter of a woman who barely escaped these ordeals, she acknowledges the intimacy to her own life of what she has sought to excavate, carried in the undertow of what she calls 'postmemory'. This is not the memory of those who actually endured collective suffering but rather the after-effects of this suffering on the second generation, the children of survivors, who 'grow up dominated by narratives that preceded their births, whose own belated stories are evacuated by the stories of the previous generation shamed by traumatic events that can be neither understood nor recreated'.

Even if resistant to understanding or recreation, these events must be rescued from silence. For Lentin, this imperative is all the greater because the historiography of the Shoah has not, in her view, given due attention either to female or child victims and because, under the black shadow of Auschwitz, this 'forgotten holocaust' has seemed hardly worthy of utterance, its survivors left 'tutored in self-silencing'. To be sure, experience in Transnistria was different from that in the Nazi death-camps — where death was generally 'quick and sanitary' and where in any case 'being a child was reason for immediate gassing'. But what infernal calculus can discount the less efficiently inflicted and hence only more long-drawn-out degradations of the Romanian deportees? In transit, a child notices 'on both sides of the road tree stumps covered in snow'; confused, she asks hesitant adults to explain. 'Only when I insisted they told me the shocking truth — these were swollen frozen human bodies from previous deportations, people who were unable to withstand the march and stayed to die by the side of the road forever'. These grisly sights could be prevented — on some convoys surviving deportees were ordered to dig a pit every ten kilometres for the corpses of those who had died from exhaustion, hunger, illness or cold (many exchanged clothes for food along the way) or those shot by Romanian sol-

diers because of their inability to keep pace. The temporary desti-
nations for Jews on these awful death pilgrimages were pigsties,
cowsheds and chicken coops where, huddled together in rags and
straw, flea-ridden and lice-infected, some died from typhus, others from hunger, exposure and dysentery. Over 50 per cent of
these deportees were children, and all about them was the death
of parents and relatives.

> Those who died were placed in the aisle and the bodies were
> stacked up until the carts arrived. . . . Meanwhile my mother
> became ill with typhus. . . . I lay beside Mother and warmed
> her with my body . . . in the morning they came and Mother
> was no longer alive.

Nor did this communal desolation annul 'small' private griefs —
being deprived through bullying or enforced barter of a cherished
possession (a necklace or pair of earrings) or abstaining from an
expedient activity (begging or theft) to honour a family code even
when one has been orphaned.

With respect to events and experiences as terrible as these,
Lentin writes of the 'impossibility of forgetting childhood
trauma'. But if the trauma cannot be forgotten, neither can it be
remembered — at least not within the 'common memory' that relates past to present in some pattern of linear chronicity. While
'postmemory' was the force that drew Lentin back to elicit and
explore these narratives of Shoah survivors, the narrators themselves, she suggests, are forever caught in a 'deep memory' that is
incapable of being assimilated into common memory. The kind of
assimilation more or less smoothly accomplished in the 'normal'
biography allows the sense of a unitary self by and in whom the
past and present are connected. Deep trauma, however, ruptures
the self at the time when it happens, and such selfhood as one
subsequently achieves cannot undo or integrate that primary rupture. And this is all the more true when the trauma happens in
childhood, a period when practice in the art of editing has not yet
armed the self in mastery of time. 'I remember the suffering, of
course, but because we were children we would also play, be-

tween death and death, between hunger and hunger, a child is a child. Therefore we absorbed it as a totality while for adults it was an episode. For children it was not an episode, it was our childhood.' While committed to the importance of producing narratives or, against an all too persistent silence, *counter*-narratives, Lentin does not believe that any later point of view for narration, whether it be an independent Israel or success in family or work, can make these narratives of child survivors into stories of 're-demption' or even of 'the triumph of the human spirit'. Apparently beyond the configuring comfort of religion or therapy, 'they tell only of rupture and death'.

Who can gainsay the judgement of those who have both experienced and deeply reflected on such trauma? But even if it remains as a kind of fateful id in survivors who can neither expunge nor appropriate it, the act of uncovering this trauma — which for the early Greek philosophers was the same as bringing it to truth — whether in speech, writing or artwork (children's most favoured medium, according to one of Lentin's sources) may at least combat its secret power, through postmemory, to pre-empt or evacuate the stories of the *next* generation. This is surely the ultimate value of telling previously untold stories, whether of the kind told by Lentin's survivors, by many of Ferriter's authors, by Smyth's protagonists in Northern Ireland, or by those before the Truth Commission in South Africa: that the very telling — always provided that truth, not propaganda or self-pity, is its primary motivation — saps their power, precisely as *un*told, to draw subsequent generations into their orbit. Whether or not there is a healing effect for the narrator, there is at least a lesson for those who come next — not that anything ensures, of course, that the latter will *learn* this lesson or assume the responsibility that it implies.

VI

Exercising responsibility in the present and for the future entails not only truthfulness about the evils of the past — and their rectification, insofar as this is humanly possible. It also requires careful

reflection on the good things that make human life worthwhile
and to which it makes sense to aspire. It may not be incongruous,
then, given the darkness of its subject, that Lentin's contribution is
followed, and this volume is concluded, by Nel Noddings's essay
on *happiness*. Happiness has always bulked large in human hopes
and dreams, it has been a major preoccupation in our philosophical tradition and, as Noddings also points out, it has often been
strongly linked with childhood: even those disinclined to romanticise the early years may still feel that 'there is something especially poignant and morally suspect about an unhappy
childhood'. Given all this, the curious fact that prompts Noddings's reflections is that *education* has so signally discounted
happiness as a goal — or has been dominated by a narrowly intellectualist conception of it that causes and legitimates a great deal
of unhappiness for very many children. Unsympathetic to the major strand of the philosophical tradition that prescribes this kind
of intellectualism, Noddings turns to recent psychological work
on 'subjective well being' (SWB), supposing that a more convinc-
ing conception of happiness may be derivable from people's reports of what actually makes them feel contented or fulfilled. But
she is then faced with the dilemma that the 'beer-guzzling couch-
potato' presents to any good liberal: while one recoils from stipu-
lating to others how they should live, one is still unable to grant
genuine respect to such a lifestyle. Nodding responds to this co-
nundrum by granting that *some* normative (or prescriptive) element is unavoidable in any credible conception of happiness; and
she goes on, with a sympathetic eye for the decencies of ordinary
life, to identify what she sees as key domains in which appropriate satisfactions make for a happy life.

Noddings identifies 'personal life' as the most important such
domain. Drawing on the work of the French philosopher Gaston
Bachelard, she locates this life primarily in the home, the first
place that inscribes itself in our bodies, 'shelters daydreaming',
and shapes our imagination and sensibility. Home opens out to a
dense, textured world of practical activities and everyday things.
This is an *inter*personal world, involving various forms of com-

panionship and care, of moral virtues and humane graces — including responsiveness to the *un*happiness of others. Not confined to domesticity or leisure, it enters the world of work and has much to do with the dignity of multifarious occupations that (despite a low prestige related by Noddings to the academic bias entrenched in education) enable or enhance the conduct of ordinary life. It is also strongly connected to *place*, reaching beyond the home to neighbourhood and region — and especially, for her, to natural landscapes and the many forms of non-human life that they support. Constituted by 'neither raw pleasure nor philosophical contemplation', this is, for Noddings, the essentially human world. In its very ordinariness, it deserves 'reverence and wonder' — which is what it receives, she suggests, in the poetry of Seamus Heaney, as well as of Whitman, Hardy, Rilke and Frost.

Noddings intends not only to sketch a conception of happiness but, more boldly, to canvass it as the proper goal of education. Happiness is, of course, importantly linked to the whole of the human lifespan, and drudgery imposed on children at school is often defended as a necessary, if unfortunate, trade-off for future, *adult* happiness — especially in terms of the kind of high-status and lucrative occupation that is seen as the prize for academic success. But, without denying the need for balance between present and future fulfilments, Noddings is offering a picture of integral human flourishing attuned to the needs of both children and adults. (As she points out, researchers of SWB find that *adults'* intuitive sense of what brings them happiness is not strongly correlated either with greater wealth, once the threshold of poverty has been comfortably passed, *or* with school success — though these two may indeed be highly correlated with each other.) When this picture is translated into an alternative agenda for schooling, it runs athwart the whole tradition of academic education and, as she recognises, 'might well threaten the status and organisation of the whole curriculum'.

It would involve a central place for home-making as a 'great art' and for an education of character orientated to caring for people and places. It would thus cut across liberal scruples about any interpenetration of public and private spheres, and counter both the intense competitiveness of schooling and the imaginative and emotional dislocation consequent on its increasing integration in a global economy that enforces mobility and endless exchangeability in 'virtual space'. It would also involve a distinctive pedagogy. Aware that happiness can hardly be planned, programmed or packaged (indeed etymology suggests that it *happens*), Noddings can see the point of wanting to keep it safe — precisely *because* one values it — from the dead hand of schooling ('I do not think schools kill curiosity and creativity in everything they do, but it is a near thing'). Still, she hopes for the possibility of a form of teaching that — perhaps like all spiritual arts — is an art of indirection; not seeking to guarantee outcomes, it can still confer 'gifts, with no strings, no tests attached', or conduct children on 'aimless but delight-filled walks in the fields of learning'. But Noddings is not just calling for pedagogical reforms that would ensure, for instance, that the 'best poetry' does not become 'poisoned' in its translation into 'school poetry'. More fundamentally, she is questioning 'the academic curriculum' and 'the traditional disciplines' as the accredited *content* of education, with the primacy they accord to 'intellectual life' and 'the pleasures of the mind'. In making this case, she has two targets simultaneously in her sights: 'academic' education itself *and* what she sees as its current entrenchment in the preparation and selection of people for high-status university courses leading in turn to highly-paid jobs and the achievement of market-defined 'happiness'. What of the very many people, she asks, who are *not* inclined towards this kind of study and will end up not in jobs of this kind but in a whole array of other sorts of work that keep our society viable? Whereas such people — still the majority even in an 'advanced' society such as the United States — can easily be regarded (and, more damagingly, can regard themselves) as failing to 'measure up' in respect of what 'really counts', from Noddings's perspective it is our present form of education that fails them. For, in persisting with a narrowly one-sided curriculum, it fails to recognise that while most people, for example, can make out very well in life with very little academic mathematics, *everybody's* happiness depends on accomplishments in home-making and companionship which schools altogether neglect.

Noddings's challenge to the traditional canons of academic education is interestingly different from most other such challenges mounted over the past two decades. Unlike post-modernist or multiculturalist critiques, for example, it does not contest universalist claims *as such*. To the contrary, from a philosophical position whose strongly pragmatist and egalitarian leanings are operative rather than stated in her essay, Noddings is herself committed to the identification of universal features of human well-being and to the consequent construction of a curriculum for *all* (albeit one susceptible of local, culture-specific modification). And while her argument can certainly be seen as an attack on the prestige of what are called 'the humanities', its motivating impulses — unlike those of many other such attacks — are themselves deeply humane. Moreover, if there is irony in her contesting the pre-eminence of intellectual life through the medium of what is itself a sophisticated intellectual exercise, this irony has a long philosophical pedigree. Many philosophers, not least Aristotle, have defended the virtues of 'plain persons' and seen them as precisely *not* deliverable by cleverness or intellectual skill. What was brutally extinguished in the Nazi 'death-camps' was just what Noddings defends as the essentially human life; and we know the extent to which heroic acts of resistance came from 'ordinary' people, while the death dealers were steeped in the best of European high culture (Lentin reminds us of Adorno's remark that there can be no poetry after Auschwitz).

If the moral intuitions that fire Noddings's argument are unimpeachable, response to her paper may concentrate on the proper role, and present reality, of education. It may be asked whether the dominant influences on contemporary schools (*and* universities) are not, on the one hand, the hard pressures of a managerialist culture whose 'performance indicators' and 'unit costs' are better adapted to technical and commercial disciplines than to the liberal arts and, on the other hand, the soft pressures of the kind of social therapeutics whose impact on curriculum is identified and criticised in Mark Morgan's essay. In face of all this, rather than putting the humanist heritage in the dock, might we still look to it for resources in helping us to respond to, and indeed to understand the direness of, our contemporary predicaments? Should home and school represent properly different kinds of world, *both* of which are badly served if they are brought too closely together? If the kind of specialised knowledge which, on Noddings's own analysis, is a prerequisite of high-status occupations in our society were *not* the concern of general education, might the mechanism through which it would then be acquired be more elitist than our public schools? And are there better ways of raising the status of the kind of occupations for which she pleads than by altering the school curriculum — for example, by ensuring that many of them are better remunerated? (Many people who fill these occupations of course are *also* interested in the 'pleasures of the mind' and in university study, and it is an honourable part of the trade union inheritance to claim access for workers to the fullness of intellectual and humanist traditions.) These are some of the questions that are prompted by Noddings's powerfully appealing perspective. However they may be answered, it is a great merit of her essay that it provokes fundamental debate about education just because — like all good philosophical writing on education since Plato — it confronts us with an alternative vision of school by also challenging our current conception of society.

A chapter on happiness may be a welcome conclusion to this book. But how is one to reconcile a plea for the centrality of happiness — even to the point of its being the proper and attainable end of education — with so many stories and accounts, in earlier chapters, of children's *un*happiness? Noddings writes as heir to an American tradition that, in its Enlightenment heyday, enshrined 'the pursuit of happiness' as a basic constitutional right. But a very different reflection on happiness is to be found in a late work of Freud's (echoed in the title of this book), *Civilisation and its Discontents*. Freud there depicts the quest for happiness as both deep-seated and impossible — frustrated inevitably by a civilisation that forces us to renounce our drives for primary satisfaction even as it protects us from the disasters that would accrue from their uninhibited pursuit. Not happiness but resignation, or tolerable misery, was the best that Freud could think to salvage from the intractable conflict between our desires and the environment (including other competing centres of will and desire) in which they must seek fulfilment, and from the even more disabling conflict, within our desires themselves, between some directed to pleasure and others directed to destruction and death. And even this stoical resignation was to be appreciated as a precarious achievement, as threatened always by inner pathology and/or outer transgression. Though this is not a pretty picture, it chimes with the insights of much great literature and has strong points of contact with the wisdom of perhaps all the great religions. And as Freud, an Austrian Jew writing when Hitler was just coming to power, could not then know — though he may have had his presentiments — it could claim terrible confirmation by the events, so vividly evoked in Lentin's essay, that were soon to engulf his own people.

It is of course the child who first falls foul of the primordial conflicts pictured by Freud. One is inclined then to ask where we can look for counter-images to his (images, as Noddings points out, are among our most enabling resources). The answer will surely be: from the great Romantic writers. From the perspective of education, Rousseau is the most obvious source, but there are also Blake, Wordsworth and Coleridge. (And these writers have precursors in English literature such as Traherne and Vaughan, as well as in earlier, more or less subterranean, religious traditions — in the Christian case traceable back to sayings of Jesus in the gospel of St. Matthew.) It is interesting that, in his genealogy of the virtual child, John Gillis omits — and thus excludes from the range of his suspicion — this Romantic inheritance. The visionary child that it imagines — the child as ecstatic explorer captivated by a prodigal world — is indeed all too easily sentimentalised and idealised (much of the literature of the nineteenth century can be read as the record of this decline). But when this image is *not* thus distorted perhaps it can inspire the kind of emancipatory and utopian perspective without which our understanding of our own condition is greatly and needlessly diminished — while at the same time it need imply no denial of the kind of conflict and suffering that Freud, among others, brings to our attention. Moreover, it may be a reverse, and no less avoidable, distortion to interpret Freud's own work as animated only by anti-idealisation. For he invites his readers (in *The Future of an Illusion*) to think of 'the depressing contrast between the radiant intelligence of a healthy child and the feeble intellectual powers of the average adult'. And Adam Philips, the general editor of a new English translation of his complete works, claims that while there is indeed a 'frustrated child at the heart of psychoanalysis — a child that has stolen the show with his anguish . . . there is another Freudian child who has been mislaid' in the subsequent development of psychoanalytic theory. This is a child 'with an unwilled relish of sensuous experience . . . a passionate love of life . . . [and] visionary qualities' — whom Philips explicitly relates to 'the legacy of romanticism' (*The Beast in the Nursery*, London, Faber and Faber, 1998, pp. 21-22).

The study of childhood, with the momentum of the two recent 'paradigm shifts' adverted to earlier in this Introduction, now seems to have fresh vigour. With a close attention to the lives of children that elicits their own voices and tracks their developing powers of agency and response, as well as historically and sociologically informed studies of the many different cultural, economic and political contexts that shape their experiences and identities, will we outgrow the 'meta-narratives' of Romanticism and psychoanalysis? From the vantage point of a different form of understanding — at once more plural and more genuinely empirical (which is to say more free of the dogmas of empiricism) — will both of these traditions seem too 'essentialist' and grandiose? Or will any study that is to do justice to the potential of childhood, and to the strength of the forces which imperil it, have to retain some nourishing contact with them — or be fated, as has so often happened in the history of ideas, to reinvent in some other guise the substance of their imagery and intuition? Perhaps these questions will cease to matter only if we enter not just a post-modern but a post-human age — powerfully imagined already in diverse genres of science fiction and increasingly presaged by new techniques in embryology and genetics — in which childhood, like much else that has long been taken as central to the human story, will have disappeared. By prompting us to raise these and many other questions, the essays collected here help us not only to guard against this eclipse but, by appreciating the gifts of our humanity, to imagine how we may better realise them.

Chapter 2

BIRTH OF THE VIRTUAL CHILD: ORIGINS OF OUR CONTRADICTORY IMAGES OF CHILDREN

John R. Gillis

'What the child *is* matters less than what we *think* it is and just why we think that way' (Kincaid, 1992).

The Victorians taught us not only what to think *about* the child but how to think *with* the child. They created the concept of 'the child' and then used it to symbolise the meaning of life itself. People have always cared and thought about particular children, and not just their own, but it was the Victorians who constructed what James Kincaid has called that 'wonderfully hollow category, able to be filled up with anyone's overflowing emotions, not least overflowing passion' (Kincaid, 1992). And we have become even more dependent on the child as a master symbol and image — so dependent that we are nearly incapable of seeing how central it is to our sense of ourselves and the world we inhabit.

The Victorians were also the first to make the child a presence in the absence of real children. They supplied western culture with a plethora of beloved child figures — innocent, pure, timeless — but they also gave us a gallery of eroticised, seductive, even savage children (Kincaid, 1992). These split images have outlived not only their progenitors but also the media that first gave them life. Figures born of books and theatre multiply in contemporary film and on television, taking on ever more fantastic forms. Victorian imaginings first colonised every segment of western society and were then exported to the rest of the world. Now, at the beginning of the twenty-first century, the west finds itself haunted by images of children that are its own creation (Stephens, 1995). Terrifying tales of street children, which were first produced in London's East End and New York's Lower East Side, are beamed back by satellite from the slums of Brazil and the Philippines to their now gentrified places of origins. These are now joined by unsettling pictures of African and Laotian boy soldiers fondling weapons they can scarcely shoulder.

In a global economy, commodified images of children circulate with ever greater velocity. One-third of all advertisements now feature children (Higgonet,1998). Politics makes similar use of their images, contributing to one of the great paradoxes of our times, namely, that western society has become an extraordinarily child-centred culture, even in the absence of children. Never have children been so valued, yet rarely have so many adults lived apart from children. Only a third of the households in the United States now contain children. Voluntary childlessness is becoming more common; and, given the longevity revolution, parents spend a smaller fraction of their lives actually living with their children. Rates of biological reproduction have been falling since the Victorian era, but what I want to call the rate of cultural reproduction has moved in exactly the opposite direction. Never have the symbols and images of the child been so pervasive. Our politics, commerce, and culture all depend on them (Holland, 1992). We are extremely attentive to these virtual children, even as we neglect, even abuse, real children. The virtual child has become so luminous that it threatens to blind us to real children.

But, while fewer adults are having children, the desire for children, often amounting to desperation, has increased not only because adult identity is still closely linked to parenthood, but also because the birth of children is felt to make a family in ways that marriage by itself cannot. When children leave home it is said of parents that 'their family has left them' (West and Patrick, 1992). Childless couples feel anamolous, and to lose a child, of whatever age, is an event so devastating that even very strong marriages may not survive it (May, 1995; Finkbeiner, 1996).

In an era when children occupy less and less real time and space, they are an ever larger presence in the land- and time-scapes of our imagination. They have been the most photographed and are now the most videoed members of our species. A half of all film stock is devoted to them — 12.5 billion snaps per year in the US alone (Higonnet, 1998; Spence and Holland, 1991). Childhood is modernity's most memorable age, but it is now also the one that is most anticipatory. 'American parents have become obsessed with raising smart, successful adults', writes Alison Gopnik. 'They have adopted the view that children matter not because of what they are but what they will grow up to be' (Gopnik, 2000).

Childhood has become modern society's myth of both origins and destiny, our explanation of who we are and what we will become. Children have assumed an iconic status, demonised as well as idolised. As Marina Warner observes, 'children have never been so visible as points of identification, as warrants of virtue, as markers of humanity'. They have become our image of origins, but, as Warner notes, 'origins are compounded of good and evil together, battling'. As the screen on which adults project their greatest hopes and deepest fears, children are imagined either as little angels or as little monsters, but rarely as just children (Warner, 1995). According to Elizabeth Goodenough:

> . . . childhood is both a chronological stage and a mental construct, an existential fact and a locus of desire, a mythical country continuously mapped by grownups in search of their subjectivity in another time and place (Goodenough, 2000).

It was during the Victorian era that 'from being the smallest and least considered of human beings, the child had become endowed with qualities that made it Godlike, fit to be worshipped and the embodiment of hope' (Cunningham, 1995). But it was also then that the child came to stand for what we find most disturbing — a symbol of forbidden sexuality, primitivism, even savagery (Kincaid, 1992; Cunningham, 1991). This split image of children, in its origins so powerfully gendered, reflected the ambivalence that adults still feel about children. The notion of innocent girls and bad boys has blurred somewhat over time, but the split image endures.

Nations and families are no longer so materially dependent on their biological offspring as they once were, but are much more dependent on them in other ways. Long before and after they have ceased to live *with* children physically, adults live *by* them culturally and psychologically. Never before in history has the symbolic connection been so intense or extended. It now begins before birth and endures beyond death, for, in the contemporary western imagination, the foetus has become the 'unborn child', while the dead or lost child haunts us in ways that no other missing person is capable of doing (Gillis, 1996; Beck and Beck-Gernsheim, 1995).

I

This paper is concerned with the way we imagine children to be, not the way they actually are. I am therefore more concerned with the culture of adults than with the culture of children, though in my conclusion I have some things to say about the latter subject. My approach owes much to Philippe Ariès, the founder of the history of childhood (Ariès, 1965). Often criticised for being too much concerned with representation, too little with actual behaviour, Ariès was right to see that the history of childhood was inseparable from that of adulthood, and not a thing in itself that can stand alone as a field of study. Starting from a more psychological perspective, Carolyn Steedman has also arrived at the conclusion that modern childhood is 'closely identified with adult selfhood'. Since the nineteenth century, every adult is required to construct a childhood appropriate to their sense of personal identity. Steedman's relational perspective thereby reconnects segments of the life course that are too often studied in isolation from one another (Steedman, 1995).

How, then, do we account for the birth of the virtual child? The first step is to be very specific with respect to its conception, in this case in the Anglo-American context. Similar developments may well be found in other north-western European societies. Indeed, the Netherlands has a strong claim to have been the first in many respects, though the value placed on the child in its Golden Age in the seventeenth century did not have the same impact as later Anglo-American developments (Kloek, forthcoming; Schama, 1987). Ariès argued that the idea of the child was already present among the elites of early modern Europe. Lawrence Stone finds similar premonitions, while Barry Levy argues that the Quakers were the progenitors of modern notions of family and childhood (Stone, 1977; Levy, 1988). Many new notions of childhood can also be seen in the Romantic movement of the late eighteenth and early nineteenth centuries. However, whatever the legitimate claims of these precursors, it was not really until the nineteenth century, and first among the Protestant Anglo-American middle strata, that these notions became hegemonic, embedded in an emerging class and gender system that would naturalise and universalise them, ultimately institutionalising them in law and social practice.

This moment coincided with the Industrial Revolution, when the household first lost its economic functions, requiring the reconstruction of family on an entirely new basis, one no longer based on material relations among its members but constituted on entirely new cultural foundations. The key to understanding the role of the Anglo-American Protestant middle classes in the invention of the virtual child lies in understanding how they coped with this change culturally as well as materially. And here the religious culture of one particular group — the Evangelicals — provides what I believe is the key to understanding this process.

The Evangelicals' obsession with sin and their agonising introspective quest for signs of divine grace set them apart not only from Catholics but also from other more conventional Protestants, who still relied on traditional religious rites and good works for reassurance of salvation. The turning point came in the mid-nineteenth century, when many Evangelicals lost faith in their belief system and turned away from institutional religion. This crisis of faith produced among them a desperate and enormously creative search for new sources of grace, a quest that turned away from introspective soul searching to find signs of salvation in the most unexpected places — in nature, among primitive peoples, but most of all, in that mythical country called childhood.

The Evangelicals had lost their faith but not their sense of sin. The Fall remained for them a central myth. Though no longer a believable historical event, it remained plausible as part of the life story. Introspection was transformed into retrospection. The Garden ceased to be a place and became a stage of life. The Fall ceased to be historical and became autobiographical. Paradise lost became childhood lost when the quest for grace turned inward and retrospective, bypassing institutional religion and finding expression within the newly sanctified realm of the family, the ultimate refuge of innocence and purity. 'God has given us each our own Paradise, our own old childhood, over which old glories linger — to which our hearts cling, as all we have ever known of Heaven upon earth', proclaimed James Anthony Froude in 1849 (Gillis, 1996).

The sacred was displaced from the realm of the supernatural to the family, with the result that, along with women, children became objects of sentimentalisation, bordering on worship. This contributed immensely to the care and protection of children, but at the cost of cloistering them from the world. Thus emerged a seminal contradiction of our times: our simultaneous worship of children and our inability to recognise them as real human beings with the faults and virtues associated with the species.

II

Just how significant this cultural revolution was can best be grasped by considering the symbolism of children in the centuries just prior to the nineteenth century. To be sure, Christian culture by then had accumulated a treasure trove of child images, stories, and myths, the most important of which centred on the Christ-child (Boas, 1966). Since the twelfth century, baby Jesus had been visual proof of divinity incarnate. But it was precisely the superabundance of heavenly children that accounts for the striking lack of images of down-to-earth children prior to the nineteenth century. Until that time, families showed little interest in images of their own children. Although there was a long tradition of family portraiture among the old elites, the Protestant middle classes were iconoclastic when it came to representations of their own family members (Gillis, 1996). Until the Victorian era, they felt no need to turn their children into symbols. Absent too were child-centred rites, such as birthdays, which we have come to regard as essential to a good family life. Christmas likewise was still a communal occasion in which children played only a small part (Nissenbaum, 1996).

With the notable exception of the seventeenth-century Dutch, childhood occupied a very small place in the pre-modern European and North American imagination. Birth was a moment to be forgotten, not remembered (Kildegaard, 1985). Indeed, people seem to have had great difficulty imagining very young children at all. The notion of the 'unborn child' was absent, but so too was the idea of the 'baby'. Children were born unaged and ungendered, if not unsexed. Naming was often delayed until after the survival of the infant was certain; and it was Christian baptism, not the physical birth itself, that marked the formal entry of the child into the world. Moreover, baptism was not yet the family celebration we understand it to be now (Gillis, 1996).

Subsequent stages of childhood were also given scant symbolic treatment. According to the Christian understanding of the journey of life, the believer drew closer to God toward the end of life. Old age was therefore the appropriate time to number one's days and to celebrate birthdays that were supposed by believers to be a sign of divine grace. By contrast, children's birthdays were rarely celebrated, and many children grew up without ever knowing their ages, for infancy and early childhood were largely undiffentiated by either age or sex. Boys' hair was allowed to grow long and they were dressed in skirts, the same as girls.

The numerical boundaries of childhood were like so many other measures of age in the pre-modern period, quite imprecise and wildly variable by class, region and gender. It was not so much how old you were as who you were that determined your place in the generational hierarchy. Early childhood often ended for boys with the ritual act of breeching; for girls, it shaded into girlhood with few visible markers. Until school and work became age-graded in the second half of the nineteenth century there was no compelling reason to remember one's age, much less celebrate it.

When adults looked back over their lives, it was not the earliest but the later years that they recounted. It was death, not birth, that gave Christian life its meaning (Porter and Porter, 1988). This was the moment when fallen humanity was reckoned to be closest to God. The dying person provided a window on immortality and therefore the deathbed was an object of fascination (Cole, 1992). By contrast, the childbed was regarded with dread, even horror, until the Victorian era. Childbirth was exclusively women's business, something that men were thankful to be relieved of and careful to distance themselves from (Gillis, 1996).

The pain mothers endured was commonly perceived as the curse of Eve, and birth itself a reenactment of The Fall, requiring that both mother and child be cleansed of its polluting effects. The rite of 'churching', meant to purify new mothers, remained in high demand until the nineteenth century (Gillis, 1996). The newborn was also regarded as a sinful polluting presence until the protective act of baptism had taken place. Even then, however, the little 'stranger' (as infants were often called) would be scrutinised for signs of original sin and disciplined in ways that we would find inappropriate for small children.

Protestants placed less faith in ritual than did Catholics, and the Evangelical middle classes of the late eighteenth and early nineteenth centuries were the most anti-ritualistic and iconoclastic of all. But their rejection of the traditional rites of churching and baptism only increased the anxiety that characterized Evangelical childrearing practices. As Philip Greven has shown, Evangelical Protestants were obsessed with issues of childish disobedience, and the most prone to resort to harsh discipline to 'bend the twig' in the proper direction (Greven, 1977; Greven, 1991).

This is not to say that the treatment of children was ever as harsh as some historians would have us believe, but neither was it careless or indulgent. Assumed to be neither particularly innocent nor particularly devilish, youngsters were not confused with either angels or demons (Walzer, 1974). As long as devils and angels were thought to be real and Christianity provided sufficiently compelling images and dramatic stories of good and evil, children carried little of the symbolic load they do today. They were neither reminders of the past nor portents of the future. Children did not signify. They were just children.

Life in a preindustrial household was noticeably lacking in the melodramatic qualities we associate with modern families. The household itself was a functional unit, and its members related to one another on an institutional rather than a sentimental basis. Household formation did not depend on natural reproduction alone, but instead incorporated unrelated persons. None of the household's members was irreplaceable. The death of a child produced grief, but the household was compelled to find a substitute and carry on. Furthermore, in a patriarchical world where fatherhood was quite separable from biological paternity and motherhood did not mean the same as biological maternity, parental identities depended on a relationship not with particular children but with all those household members entrusted to their care (Gillis, 1996).

III

The effects of the Industrial Revolution of the mid-nineteenth century differed by class and region, but perhaps the most affected was the middle-class household, whose functions and composition were profoundly altered when production was removed to the factory and the office. While middle-class households continued to contain unrelated persons as domestic servants well into the twentieth century, a clear distinction was now made between them and the biologically constituted nuclear family. For the first time, fatherhood became exclusively associated with biological paternity and motherhood with biological maternity. The way was now cleared for a corresponding redefinition of childhood as an irreplaceable relationship between a specific parent and a specific child, drawing, for the first time, a sharp line between so-called 'natural' offspring and adopted or fostered children.

Removal of production from the household transformed the meaning of fatherhood, limiting it to the breadwinner role, but it likewise changed motherhood, transforming it into an all-consuming identity, something transcending the act of mothering. Mothers became the symbolic centres of middle-class families at the moment when fathers were recast as strangers to the domestic realm. The mother's real and symbolic involvement with the individual child was simultaneously transformed, intensified in a manner that ultimately made smaller numbers of children attractive and led to fertility control (Gillis, 1992). Simultaneously, the definition of family narrowed to the nuclear unit, defined by the presence of children born to it (Griswold, 1993; Gillis, 1996).

It was at this same moment that the cultural understanding of the child underwent a revolution which was to have an immense impact on the ideas and practices of modern family life. Birth and death changed places, and it was newborns who were now the window on eternity. Infants were, wrote Wordsworth, 'fresh from the hand of God, living blessings which have drifted down to us from the imperial palace of the love of God' (Cunningham, 1995). It was at this moment that among the middle classes birth ceased to be a symbolic reenactment of The Fall and became a sacred moment, a kind of secular sacrament. The birthing room was no longer the exclusive domain of women; it was made accessible to fathers, with middle-class men becoming the first fathers to attend the birth of their children. These men found birth as personally redemptive as their wives found it personally sanctifying (Gillis, 1996).

Although working-class women continued to use the rite of churching, the middle classes, who now regarded birth itself as purifying, abandoned it entirely. Infant baptism lost its original meaning and became the modern christening ceremony, a family occasion celebrating birth itself. Naming no longer waited on the survival of the infant and the child's birthday took on great symbolic importance for the first time (Gillis, 1996). The child was now a luminous presence, itself a symbol of innocence, purity, a source of sacredness that the Christian churches were quick to recognise as a source of institutional revitalisation. In the second half of the nineteenth century religious ceremonies of Judaism as well as Christianity became increasingly family- and child-centred, a recognition of the shifting locus of the sacred (Joselit, 1994).

It is important to understand, however, that children were still born into the world unaged and ungendered. The notion of 'baby' did not make its way into the medical literature and popular consciousness until the very end of the century (Wright, 1987). Boys and girls continued to be treated and dressed the same, and the rites of breeching lost none of their significance until the early twentieth century. Men continued to remember this as the moment of their expulsion from the Garden of Delights (Robson, 2001). There was no symbolic counterpart for girls, no end to their age of innocence.

For boys, growing up meant not only putting away childish things but distancing themselves from everything feminine. For girls it meant appropriating the fullness of their femininity. Thus, for men childhood came to be associated with something left behind. And it was these same men who now set about constructing childhood as something 'retrospective, and feminized, rather than as anticipatory, and masculinized' (Robson, 2001). Hence the Victorian tendency, shaped primarily by male writers, artists and photographers, to represent the ideal child as the little girl and the juvenile delinquent as the bad boy (Robson, 2001). Gender was so inseparable from the image of the child that for a very long time we have failed to detect this dimension. Today, we ignore it at enormous risk to our understanding both of modern childhood and modern adulthood.

IV

By the end of the nineteenth century, childhood had become what Hugh Cunningham has called a 'substitute religion', but one recognisably Judeo-Christian in its elements. Childhood stood for the Garden of Eden, no longer a place but a stage in the journey of life that led inevitably to the fallen state of adulthood (Cunningham, 1991). It is little wonder that childhood had by this time become an object of intense nostalgia, attracting to itself all those longings that had previously attached themselves to the Garden itself (Degler, 1980; Pollock, 1983; Kincaid, 1992). Childhood had come to symbolise not only uncorrupted nature but also the nobility associated with simpler times and peoples. This displacement coincided with New Imperialism, which terminated the myth of the noble savage. Once the entire globe had been explored and all hope of finding actual earthly paradise was exhausted, the child became the final repository of the visions of unbounded happiness that had been sought by Europeans for centuries (Cunningham, 1991). But, at the same time, Europeans found their demons coming home to roost. This was the moment when the hyper-masculinised juvenile delinquent was born, the embodiment of the primitive in what many were coming to see as an overly feminised civilisation. 'The construction of the ideal inevitably spawns its opposite', observes Catherine Robson (Robson, 2001). The monstrous haunts the angelic, a classic example of the return of the repressed.

By 1900 childhood had displaced old age as the most memorable part of the lifetime. Autobiographical writings dwelt increasingly on early childhood experiences, while a whole new set of commemorative practices developed to allow adult males access not only to their own childhood memories, but, perhaps more important, to children, who were increasingly seen as mnemonic resources, the repository of the earliest memories of mankind itself. With late nineteenth-century evolutionary theory came the notion that each individual recapitulated the history of the human species. Thus the child was the closest thing to early man, the repository of unspoiled qualities, but also a potential source of primitive instincts, even savagery (Cunningham, 1991).

Such ideas found expression in science and in the emerging family cultures of the period. The middle-class festive calendar came to revolve increasingly around children, and times of renewal when adults (especially men) grown weary of the urban industrial world, could return to simpler, purer things. The newly invented, secularised family Christmas was thought of in precisely those terms, as a moment when men could reconnect not only with children but with their own childhoods. As the Englishman, Clement Miles, remarked:

> At no time in the world's history has so much been made of children as today, and because Christmas is their feast its lustre continues unabated in an age when dogmatic Christianity has largely lost its hold. . . . Christmas is the feast of beginnings, of instinctive, happy childhood (Miles, 1912; Gillis, 1996).

It was no longer the end but the beginning that now gave life its meaning. The precious glimpse of immortality previously associated with the deathbed was relocated to the cradle, but, as Anne Higonnet observes, the image of little angels

> stows away a dark side: a threat of loss, of change, and ultimately, of death. Romantic images of childhood gain power not only from their charm, but also from their menace (Higonnet, 1998).

Photographs were already becoming the Victorians' way of warding off death. Their albums are full of dead children, posed either as living or as sleeping, scarcely distinguishable from their living brothers and sisters. As a subject, the dead child did not fall out of favour until the twentieth century (Burns, 1990; Douglass, 1977; Zelizer, 1985; Martin-Fugier, 1990; Kildegaard, 1985).

Here again the gender dimension is very important. Most of the early photographers of children were older men of the world, endowed by this new technology with the representational power previously possessed only by artists, enabling them to capture a living moment and to consign it to eternity. Catherine Robson has argued (plausibly, I think) that this constituted for them a kind of psychological recovery project, restoring something of their 'lost' feminine self through capturing the pristine image of the little girl (Robson, 2001). Along with other Victorian cultural practices, such as children's birthdays and Christmas, this allowed them access to the longed-for world of innocence denied them by their gender.

Today, little girls are less likely to be icons of lost innocence (Higonnet, 1998). In the twentieth century, they too were expelled from the Garden. Girls are more likely to be protected than boys, but of late they have been haunted by their own demons. With rising female crime rates, it is easy enough to conjure ever more troubling images of female delinquency. However, little boys have not taken on the mantle of innocence. Male children are no longer dressed as girls and the rites of breeching have long since been abandoned. Yet family and home are still gendered feminine, something that boys must distance themselves from if they are to become 'real men'. The mythical country of childhood remains strange to men, who continue to be significanly more nostalgic than do women (Gillis, 1996).

Photographing little girls as angels may have gone out of fashion, but we still seek those traces of immortality in baby pictures, and, most recently, on those ultrasound images that give us ultimate access to images of humanity untainted by the passage of time. As Susan Sontag has suggested, the photograph remains our means of glimpsing eternity, holding time at bay (Sontag, 1972). But in this age of the 'hurried child', when children are not allowed to linger even in their infancy, the sonogram of the 'unborn child' has become for many the ultimate symbol of immortality. It has the advantage over the photograph that it is exempt from the imperfections of life itself. The image of the foetus provides all those qualities that western culture has projected onto childhood since the mid-nineteenth century. In effect, the womb has become the Garden and the foetus the latest little angel, making abortion seem to some the work of the devil, and the women who exercise this choice Eve incarnate (Rothman, 1989; Stolberg, 1998; Lundin and Akesson, 1996).

V

Over the past twenty years or so the obstacles to family formation have multiplied. The age of marriage rises, child-bearing is postponed and the number of childless couples increases. There are fewer children, but contemporary society has become increasingly obsessed not just with lost children whose images appear in posters and on milk cartons but also, if the recent spate of books on the disappearance of childhood is any indication, with losing childhood altogether (Postman, 1992; Sommerville, 1982; Winn, 1984; Kotlowitz, 1991). As Paula Fass has noted:

> That dream of personal resurrection — to live once more through our children — has made them dearer to us, while their loss has become all the more unbearable, to outlive them, a modern curse (Fass, 1997).

And so in this new century the pace of iconisation, ritualisation, and mythologisation of childhood quickens. Children bear a double symbolic burden, however. They must stand not only for a lost past, but an elusive future. We want to see in them the adults we would like ourselves to be. The Victorians may have erred in keeping children too long in childhood; we make the mistake of propelling them too early into adulthood. But, of course, we remain wary of precocity, and are overprotective even as we attempt to turn children into smart adults. The contemporary child, long since isolated from nature, and no longer allowed access to the street, inhabits a series of worlds — the day-care centre, kindergarten, the playground, the summer camp — purpose-built to satisfy adult hopes and allay adult fears, but not always serving the best interests of children (Nahban and Trimble, 1994).

As adult relations with children become increasingly mediated by images, rituals, and highly advertised products, the social as well as the material costs mount. For children, the price is the loss of autonomy. I am not confident in judging whether children behave worse or better now, but it is clear that children today lead increasingly scripted lives. And when they do not conform to adult idealisations, they are perceived as fallen angels or, worse, little monsters. As John Demos has argued, in a situation where adult identities are so dependent on idealised notions of parent/child relations, childish misbehaviour becomes especially threatening, producing anger and violence directed toward otherwise beloved children (Demos, 1986; Beck and Beck-Gernsheim, 1995).

Our attempt to live by the icon of the child makes it all the more difficult to live with real children. Alison Gopnik suggests that we should stop thinking about children as potential and take what she calls the 'intrinsic view — the view that childhood and caring for children are valuable in and of and for themselves' (Gopnik, 2000). Indeed, we have to become aware of the way our cultural constructions, once reified, blind rather than enlighten us to the true nature of our relations with children. We need to invent new images and find different stories to tell ourselves, but, most important, we need to attend to those conditions that make adulthood itself so problematic and produce the longings that are projected onto children. We might start by heeding Marina Warner's caution that, 'without paying attention to adults and their circumstances, children cannot begin to meet the hopes and expectations of our torn dreams about what a child and childhood should be' (Warner, 1995). Paying more heed to adult needs would in the long run be of great benefit not only to us but to our children.

References

Ariès, Philippe (1965). *Centuries of Childhood*. New York: Vintage.

Beck, Ulrich and Beck-Gernsheim, Elisabeth (1995). *The Normal Chaos of Love* (trans. Mark Ritter and Jane Wiebel). Cambridge: Polity.

Boas, George (1966). *The Cult of Childhood*. London: Warburg Institute.

Britain and Her Birth Rate (1945). London: Murray.

Burns, Stanley (1990). *Sleeping Beauty: Memorial Photography in America*. Altedena, California: Twelve Trees Press.

Busfield, Joan & Paddon, Michael (1977). *Thinking about Children: Sociology and Fertility in Post-war England*. Cambridge: Cambridge University Press.

Cole, Thomas (1992). *The Journey of Life: A Cultural History of Aging in America*. Cambridge: Cambridge University Press.

Cross, Gary (1997). *Kid's Stuff: Toys and the Changing World of American Childhood*. Cambridge: Harvard University Press.

Cunningham, Hugh (1991). *The Children of the Poor: Representations of Childhood since the Seventeenth Century*. Oxford: Blackwell.

Cunningham, Hugh (1995). *Children and Childhood in Western Society since 1500*. London: Longman.

Degler, Carl (1980). *At Odds: Women and the Family in America from the Revolution to the Present*. New York: Oxford.

Demos, John (1986). *Past, Present, and Personal: The Family and the Life Course in America*. New York: Oxford.

Douglass, Ann (1977). *The Feminization of American Culture*. New York: Knopf.

Fass, Paula (1997). *Kidnapped: Child Abduction in America*. New York: Oxford.

Finkbeiner, Ann K. (1996). *After the Death of a Child: Living with Loss through the Years*. New York: Free Press.

Furstenberg, Frank and Cherlin, Andrew (1986). *The New American Grandparenthood: A Place in the Family, a Life Apart*. New York: Basic.

Gillis, John R. (1992). 'Gender and fertility decline among the British middle classes' in John Gillis, Louise Tilly and David Levine (eds) *The European Experience of Declining Fertility, 1850–1970*. Oxford: Blackwell.

Gillis, John R. (1996). *A World of Their Own Making: Myth, Ritual, and the Quest for Family Values*. New York: Basic.

Goodenough, Elizabeth (2000). 'Introduction' to special issue on the Secret Spaces of Childhood, *Michigan Quarterly Review*, 29, No. 2.

Gopnik, Alison (2000). 'Children need childhood, not vocational training' in *The New York Times*, 24 December.

Greven, Philip (1977). *The Protestant Temperament: Patterns of Childrearing, Religious Experience, and the Self in Early America*. New York: Knopf.

Greven, Philip (1991). *Spare the Child: The Religous Roots of Punishment and the Psychological Impact of Physical Abuse*. New York: Knopf.

Griswold, Robert (1993). *Fatherhood in America: A History*. New York: Basic.

Higgonet, Anne (1998). *Pictures of Innocence: The History and Crises of Ideal Childhood*. London: Thames and Hudson.

Holland, Patricia (1992). *What is a Child? Popular Images of Childhood*. London: Virago.

Joselit, Jenna W. (1994). *The Wonders of America: Reinventing Jewish Culture, 1880–1950*. New York: Hill and Wang.

Kildegaard, Bjarne (1985). 'Unlimited memory: Photography and the differentiation of familial intimacy', *Ethnologia Scandinavica*, Vol. 15, pp. 71–89.

Kincaid, James (1992). *Child-loving: The Erotic Child and Victorian Culture*. New York: Routledge.

Kloek, Els (forthcoming). '"The Dutch Case": A critical survey of the history of childhood in the early modern time in the Netherlands, ca 1500–1800' in W. Koops and M. Zuckerman (eds), *The Century of the Child*.

Kotlowitz, A. (1991). *There Are No Children Here*. New York: Doubleday.

Levy, Barry (1988). *Quakers and the American Family: British Settlement in the Delaware Valley*. New York: Oxford.

Lundin, Susanne, and Lynn Akesson (1996). 'Creating life and explaining death', *Ethnologia Europea*, Vol. 26.

Martin-Fugier, Anne (1990). 'Bourgeois rituals' in Michelle Perrot (ed.) *A History of Private Life*, Vol. 5. Cambridge; Harvard University Press.

May, Elaine Tyler (1995). *Barren in the Promised Land: Childless Americans and the Pursuit of Happiness*. New York: Basic.

Miles, A. Clement (1912). *Christmas in Ritual and Tradition, Christian and Pagan*. London: T. Fisher Unwin.

Nahban, Gary Paul and Stephen Trimble (1994). *The Geography of Childhood: Why Children Need Wild Places*. Boston: Beacon.

Nissenbaum, Stephen (1996). *The Battle for Christmas*. New York: Knopf.

Pollock, Linda (1983). *Forgotten Children: Parent–Child Relations from 1500 to 1900*. Cambridge: Cambridge University Press.

Porter, Roy and Porter, Dorothy (1988). *In Sickness and in Health: The British Experience, 1650–1850*. Oxford: Blackwell.

Postman, Neil (1992). *The Disappearance of Childhood*. 2nd ed. New York: Vintage.

Robson, Catherine (2001). *Men in Wonderland: The Lost Girlhood of Victorian Gentleman*. Princeton: Princeton University Press.

Rothman, Barbara Katz (1989). *Recreating Motherhood: Ideology and Technology in Patriarchal Society*. New York: W.W. Norton.

Ruby, Jay (1995). *Secure the Shadow: Death and Photography in America*. Cambridge: MIT Press.

Schama, Simon (1987). *The Embarrassment of Riches: An Interpretation of Dutch Culture in the Golden Age*. New York: Knopf.

Sommerville, John (1982). *The Rse and Fall of Childhood*. Beverly Hills: Sage.

Sontag, Susan (1972). *On Photography*. New York: Delta.

Spence, Jo and Holland, Patricia (1991). *Family Snaps: The Messages of Domestic Photography*. London: Virago.

Steedman, Carolyn (1995). *Strange Dislocations: Childhood and the Idea of Human Interiority*. London: Virago.

Stearns, Peter (forthcoming). 'Historical perspectives on 20th-century American childhood' in W. Koops and M. Zuckerman (eds) *The Century of the Child*.

Stephens, Sharon (1995). 'Introduction: Children and the politics of culture in late capitalism' in Sharon Stephens (ed.) *Children and the Politics of Culture*. Princeton: Princeton University Press.

Stolberg, Sheryl Gay (1998). 'Shifting certainties in the abortion war'. *The New York Times*, January 11.

Stone, Lawrence (1977). *The Family, Sex, and Marriage in England, 1500-1800*. New York: Harper & Row.

Walzer, John F. (1974). 'A period of ambivalence: Eighteenth-century American childhood' in Lloyd de Mause (ed.) *The History of Childhood*. New York: Psychohistory Press.

Warner, Marina (1995). *Six Myths of Our Time: Little Angels, Little Monsters, Beautiful Beasts and more*. New York: Vintage.

West, Elliott and Petrick, Paula (eds) *Small Worlds: Children and Adolescence in America, 1850-1950*. Lawrence: University of Kansas Press.

Winn, Maria (1984). *Children without Childhood*. Harmondsworth: Penguin.

Wright, Peter (1987). 'The social construction of babyhood: The definition of infant care as a medical problem' in A. Bryman, et al. (eds) *Rethinking the Life Cycle*. London: Macmillan.

Chapter 3

THE COSMOPOLITAN FAMILY: SOCIAL ADAPTATION TO A CHANGING WORLD

David Elkind

INTRODUCTION

The family is a social organism and society is its natural habitat. When that habitat changes, so must the family. In the usual order of things, adaptation to change comes about gradually by natural variation and selection of the fittest. When environmental change is very rapid, however, this process is disturbed, and the dynamic equilibrium between the family and the social environment is upset. Over the past half-century the rapidity of social and technological change has disrupted the equilibrium between family and society. The once predominant nuclear family is now but one among many family forms vying for selection as the most suitable to the postmodern, post-industrial world.

The contemporary disequilibrium between family and society results from the extraordinary changes in social values, roles and perceptions that have marked our entry into postmodernity. The modern nuclear family — two parents, one staying home to keep house and to rear the children — has assimilated the conservative values, rigid role definitions and romanticised conceptions of parents, children and youth of the late modern society. The postmodern cosmopolitan family — two parents working, single-parent, remarried, adoptive and other families — has, to varying degrees, assimilated the liberal values, the overlapping role definitions and practical perceptions of children and youth of the postmodern world.

From an evolutionary standpoint, the emergence of a diversity of family forms is to be expected in response to the new demands of a changed social habitat. Given the new societal spectrum, a variety of family forms is the prerequisite to the eventual selection of the most adaptive child-rearing configuration. The nuclear family was, perhaps, the most adaptive family form for the society created by the Industrial Revolution. It may well be, however, that this family form is no longer the best suited to meet the demands of the postmodern era. We may have to accept either a variety of family forms, or a new family form, as the modal pattern for postmodern societies.

In the meantime, there will be a period — the one we are in now — where the less adaptive forms have yet to be selected out. In this essay, I will describe the values, roles and perceptions of the cosmopolitan family forms that have become more numerous than the once predominant nuclear family. I will be concerned particularly with the fact that many of these emergent family forms, at least during this transitional period, place undue hardships on children and youth. For purposes of exposition, I will compare the adaptations of the modern *nuclear* family with those of the postmodern *cosmopolitan* family. I will, however, limit myself to examples from the United States, the society I know best. Families in other countries may be either ahead or behind the US with respect to the ascendance of the cosmopolitan family. Finally, I do not mean to pass value judgements. Looked at as an organism, the family's attempts to meet the demands of a new social milieu are not bad or good, right or wrong, but rather adaptive efforts to reconcile the needs of the family with the demands of the larger society.

FROM THE PROVINCIAL TO THE COSMOPOLITAN FAMILY

Modern American society, which lasted roughly from the late nineteenth to the middle of the twentieth century, might be characterised as *provincial*. It was conservative in its social values, in its clearly articulated sexual and occupational roles, and in its romanticised perceptions of parents, children and youth. In contrast, our postmodern society is best described as *cosmopolitan*; it is a worldly admixture, or *pastiche*, of liberal cultural values, of blended sexual and occupational roles, and of the practical perceptions of parents, children and youth. The family forms that I have described as cosmopolitan have assimilated, to varying degrees, these facets of cosmopolitan society.

THE MODERN NUCLEAR FAMILY

Values

The modern nuclear family was nicely adapted to the provincial society. It assimilated the conservative values, particularly that of a shared American ethos, exemplified in the metaphor of the 'melting pot'. Yet despite, or perhaps because of, that prescribed common ethos, racial, ethnic and religious identities created hard and fast boundaries. Marriage outside of one's group, for example, often meant estrangement from both family and friends. Conservative marriage values prevailed, and divorced, single-parent, and two-parent working families were either pitied or vilified. A similar conservatism held in relation to sexual matters. There was overt censorship of sexuality in the media. For example, Henry Miller's *Tropic of Cancer*, published in Paris in 1934, was immediately banned by US customs officials on the grounds of obscenity.

Roles

The roles for men and women were quite distinct and this was regarded as an evolutionary trend. Harvard sociologist Tallcott Parsons (1951) theorised that as society evolved it was character-

ised by role differentiation. In his view, specialisation was a necessary prerequisite to societal efficiency. Indeed, 'efficiency' was
the mantra of the late modern era. The nuclear family was the
most efficient and therefore the most advanced from an evolutionary perspective. Husbands were the 'good providers' (Bernard, 1981, p. 36) and wives were the 'housewives' (Matthews,
1987), who ran the household and reared the children. Women
were also expected to uphold the moral standards of society. The
Prohibition movement of the early twentieth century was primarily the work of women asserting their role as the guardians of the
moral order.

Parent Perceptions

Until about the middle of the twentieth century, perceptions of
parents and their children were romanticised. Men and women
were thought to have an inborn disposition for child-rearing that
was aroused whenever a couple had children. As Donal Winnicott, the English paediatrician and analyst, put it: 'You are a good
enough parent, you don't have to take classes or get a degree, just
use your common sense and you will do fine' (Winnicott, 1987).
Famed American paediatrician Benjamin Spock gave similar advice in his classic book *Baby and Child Care* (Spock, 1976). He too
told parents to rely on their own intuition and good judgement.

During this period, those who wrote for parents sought to
help them fully realise their natural parenting inclinations by giving them information about the norms of growth and development. Paediatrician Arnold Gesell, for example, gave detailed descriptions of the language, social and emotional development of
children at successive age levels. He portrayed the six-year-old as
always talking, always eating, constantly moving and very self-
centred. By seven these traits were a bit more subdued and became even quieter by age eight. By age nine, children were even a
little introverted.

At age ten, however, children brought it all together. They had
had enough life experience to feel comfortable about themselves

as children, to like their family, their friends, their teachers, and were even able to tolerate, within limits, their siblings. Gesell, however, cautioned parents not to become complacent. Those wonderfully rounded ten-year-olds turned eleven and then twelve. And at that age, parents, who before could do no wrong, now could do no right. From their twelve-year-olds, parents often heard the refrain: 'You don't know how to talk, walk, or to dress, and I don't want to be seen with you in public' (Gesell and Illg, 1943).

It should be said that the perception of parenting as an inborn disposition that appears when we have children had an additional adaptive function. First, it reinforced the nuclear family value that it was only the mother who could, or should, rear young children. A necessary correlate of that value, however, was that non-parents were not capable of caring for and educating young children. There was thus a bias against non-parental care of young children. It is certainly true that kindergartens became popular at the turn of the twentieth century. Yet, it is also the case that these programmes were regarded as merely providing play opportunities and socialisation experiences for children. They were not regarded as having any child-rearing or educational value or significance.

Child Perceptions

The dominant perception of children in the late modern age — from about the end of the nineteenth century to the middle of the twentieth — was that of *innocence*. During this period a new humanitarian sensibility became widespread across Europe and America. Alfred Binet created the intelligence test to assess those of low mental ability so that they could get the special education they required. Freud's theory of the neuroses suggested that mental disorders were medical conditions and not the work of the devil or evil spirits. The scientific study of children came into its own with the publication of G. Stanley Hall's two volumes on adolescence. These considerations, coupled with the prevalence of universal, free public education, gave children and adolescents a unique definition, that of the pupil or student. This special status was formalised by child labour and compulsory schooling legislation that set childhood and adolescence apart from adulthood.

Although the conservative values and strict role constraints of the nuclear family were often hard upon parents, they were well suited to the needs of children. Children are not born social. Becoming social means, in large part, learning to control one's impulses and desires, and to respect and value the needs, feelings and interests of others. Socialisation transpires more easily when values and roles are clear and well articulated than when they are relative and overlapping. The social taboos and legal barriers to divorce thus prevented a severe source of child stress. A family adaptation such as the nuclear family may be better suited therefore to the needs of children than it is to the needs of parents.

One measure of the fit between the society and the perception of the child is the extent to which society encourages and supports the perpetuation of child culture. The culture of childhood — the toys, games, jokes, sayings and rituals created by children and passed down by oral tradition — flourished in the late modern era. The creation of a unique and protected role for children gave them time to play. And play they did. Children were on the streets and on empty lots engaging in their own games, or their own versions of adult sports. Access to the culture of childhood was open to all children. Learning the popular games, toys, jokes and riddles was all that was required of a child to gain acceptance by their peers. Engaged in child culture, children learned to respect each other and to honour the social hierarchies of their peer group. Although the culture of childhood has always been present to some extent, it came into its own under the late modern perception of childhood innocence.

Perceptions of Adolescents

Adolescents in the late modern era were perceived as immature and in need of adult guidance and direction. While it was recognised that young people might get into trouble, this was looked upon as part of a healthy experimentation and a 'sowing of wild oats' before settling down to adult occupations and responsibilities. To aid young people find their path, there were many adult organised clubs in both schools and the larger community. These programmes provided both moral and intellectual guidance and support for young people. While there was not a culture of adolescence in the same sense as there is for childhood, there was an apprenticeship period that provided young people with limits, guidance and direction during their passage to adulthood.

THE POSTMODERN COSMOPOLITAN FAMILY

Many different events helped to bring about a sea change in the habitat of American society that has been called postmodernity: two world wars, the Holocaust, the atomic bomb, the women's and civil rights movements, the sexual revolution and the technological innovations that made high culture (classical music, theatre and art) and world travel generally accessible. Postmodernism challenged the notion of superior values, of clearly defined gender roles as well as the romantic perceptions of parents, children and adolescents. It was not so much a revolt against their values, roles and perceptions as a critique of their failure to value diversity, role flexibility and real as opposed to romantic perceptions.

The civil rights movement made public the bias and prejudice hidden in the ethos of the melting pot. This movement can be credited with gaining equal educational and occupational opportunities for people of colour. It also helped to make Americans recognise, appreciate and value the contributions of minorities to science, literature, the arts, as well as to our military victories. In its turn, the women's movement effectively deconstructed the once rigid gender roles and opened the educational and vocational doors once closed to women. For its part the sexual revolution made sex a mutually agreed upon and mutually satisfying activity, rather than a man's pleasure and a woman's burden. In doing so it helped to break down the romantic perceptions of parents (who presumably never engaged in sex other than to procreate) and of children and youth (who were not supposed to be interested in this activity).

Postmodern cosmopolitan families have, to varying degrees, accommodated these postmodern critiques. Nuclear families, two-parent working, blended (divorced and remarried), single, adoptive, and mixed racial families are today recognised, and valued, as acceptable child-rearing options. The roles of mother and father now overlap. Many mothers work outside the home and fathers play a greater role in homemaking and in child-rearing. Likewise, the perceptions of parents, children and adolescents have changed, adapting to the demands of the post-industrial information age.

Cosmopolitan Values

The once-vaunted 'melting pot' ethos of the modern era has been replaced by the acceptance and valuation of racial, cultural and ethnic differences. Interestingly, as we have given up a common social ethos as a matter of social policy, we are moving closer to it in actuality. Intermarriage among those of different religious, racial and ethnic groups is much more common and much more accepted than it was during the modern era. There is now a much greater social acceptance of divorce, of gay and lesbian relationships, of single parenting and of premarital cohabitation. Sexual values have been transformed as well. With the social acceptance of premarital sex, virginity has lost its value. It can no longer be traded in, as it once was, for a promise of fidelity on the part of the husband. Censorship of the media has all but disappeared. *Tropic of Cancer* — finally available in the United States in the 1960s — quickly became a bestseller.

Cosmopolitan Roles

As in the case of provincial values, the solidly defined social roles of the modern era have given way to the more permeable and less rigid roles of postmodernity. Women are no longer relegated solely to the housewife, nuturing-mother role. Today, women are free to enter all occupations and currently more than 50 per cent of those entering American medical schools are women. To be sure, balancing home and career is a challenge, and often a necessity rather than a matter of choice. Nonetheless, pursuing a professional career was an option unavailable to most women of earlier generations. Male roles have not changed much, but men today are permitted to be sensitive and compassionate, and are expected to participate in both homemaking and child-rearing.

Perceptions of Parents

Parents' perceptions of themselves are often taken, in part, from the way they are presented in wider society. During the modern era, parents were portrayed in television programmes and in films as caring, thoughtful and wise. They inevitably had rewarding solutions for all of their children's difficulties. And the difficulties were the perennial child problems such as sibling rivalry, selfishness, dishonesty and the like. After mid-century, however, the portrayal of parents changed and, increasingly, dysfunctional families became the rule both on television programmes and in films. In many of these series, such as *The Simpsons*, the children are depicted as brighter than the adults — or at least the bumbling fathers. The perception that parents are inept and in need of professional help is reflected in the outpouring of parenting magazines, books, tapes and workshops.

As a result of this societal portrayal, many contemporary parents now accept this perception of their own *ineptitude*. Some parents respond to this perception by looking to experts for parenting techniques that will help them to discipline their children. Others simply accept their ineptitude and treat their children as equals who, in effect, do not need parenting. Those parents who do feel competent to rear their children without expert help are nonetheless often at odds with other parents. They have to defend their decisions about not letting their children go along with the crowd, not over-scheduling them, and giving them time for themselves.

It is important to point out that the perception of parental ineptitude, like that of parenting as inborn disposition, serves societal needs. The perception of parental ineptitude suggests that child-rearing can be learned and that you do not have to be a parent to acquire parenting skills. This has made possible the acceptance of shared parenting — the idea that parenting can be given over, in part at least, to non-familial care-givers — without doing harm to the child. When parenting is regarded as a learned technique, rather than a biological disposition, it frees parents to entrust the care and education of young children to non-familial care-givers. This is a major accommodation of the cosmopolitan family.

The Cosmopolitan Child

The perception of children in the postmodern era has changed from one of innocence to one of competence. Not surprisingly, this changed conception was an adaptation to the demands of postmodern society. The idea of competence was introduced to acknowledge the accommodations imposed upon cosmopolitan children. These accommodations are of three types: *exchange* in the realm of values; *addition and subtraction* with respect to roles; and *novelty* in regard to their abilities.

With respect to values, children no less than parents have to deal with the perception of parental ineptitude and the acceptance of non-familial child-rearing. In effect, young children have been required to forgo the comfort of being home-reared for the communal stimulation of the day-care centre. There is no question that childcare centres can be warm and welcoming and that non-parental caregivers can manage children. Nor is it the case that a mother by staying at home to care for her young children will necessarily do a better job than a good childcare centre. The problem is that, in the United States at least, the overall quality of centre-based care is not yet at the level of overall home care.

It is important to recognise that the acceptance of non-parental childcare, by children as well as their parents, is critical for an information society. In the information age, the abilities and talents of women are very much in demand. Consequently, in today's world women, including mothers of young children, work. That is a societal given and the exchange of home care for out-of-home care is an adaptation young children must make to this new reality. The perception of young children as competent to cope with such care is a necessary, complementary accommodation.

With regard to addition/subtraction, the culture of childhood has been largely subtracted from the lives of cosmopolitan children. There are many different reasons for this. For one thing, the environment is no longer as safe as it was even a few decades ago. Contemporary parents are hesitant to tell their children to go out and play when there are few open areas, when cars are numerous and powerful, and when violence is an ever-present threat. Moreover, the new information and global economies have made parents aware of the importance of education for success in today's society. The idea that education is a race, and that the sooner you start the greater your chances of success, has become a mantra for many parents. Free time, once available for engaging in the culture of childhood, is now spent taking lessons, going to after-school tutoring, and doing homework. As a result, much of the culture of childhood is disappearing.

If the culture of childhood has been subtracted from the life of today's children, something else has been added. This is the fabricated child culture of the media and merchandisers. The culture of Pokemon, the Sony Playstation, Nintendo 64 and Barbie have all but eclipsed the games, jokes, riddles, jump-rope songs, hop-scotch rhymes that once occupied children. In the United States at least, the culture of childhood has become a fabricated consumer culture created to sell products to children. Too often, these products are unhealthy. In the United States there has been a 50 per cent increase in obesity among children largely as a result of eating junk food while watching television.

The rationale for replacing the spontaneous culture of childhood with the fabricated culture of consumerism is once again the perception of child competence. Children are, it is assumed, com-

petent to deal with advertisements and to make accurate judgements as to their truthfulness and reliability. This is a good example of maladaptation. The perception of child competence that is
adaptive in the realm of childcare becomes maladaptive when it is
inappropriately transferred to another social realm. Children may
well be competent to deal with non-parental care, but they are less
competent to deal with advertising strategies that use their imma-
turity against them.

A further sense in which the postmodern child is seen as competent is more positive. The appearance of the new information
technologies has released potentials of child adaptive competence
that would never have been realised in earlier eras. Computers
have enabled many handicapped children to communicate in
ways that were never possible before. For those with limited and
partial sight, there are now machines that will read text to them so
that they no longer have to be read to, or to use braille. For those
of limited hearing there are new prescription hearing aids programmed to fit the pattern of hearing loss. Many physically challenged children can have, thanks to computers, means of communication never before available to them. Technologies help many
children with special needs to lead happier and more productive
lives than was possible in the past.

Unfortunately, the positive benefits of technology have their
flip side. In the United States the fastest growing educational
software is so-called Lapware, computer programmes for infants
from six months to two years of age. Such programmes have little
to commend them and feed upon parental anxieties and concerns
rather than upon the social, intellectual and emotional needs of
children. Once again we see an accommodation that is adaptive in
one social domain being misused and abused in another. We must
hope that the maladaptive accommodations will not survive.

The Cosmopolitan Adolescent

It is important to keep in mind, while describing the cosmopolitan
adolescent, that young people today are still very much like ear-

lier generations in many important respects. Adolescents today must still go through the many perils of puberty, the shock of peer group isolation, disillusionment and betrayal, and the struggle to create a personal identity that will provide them with a sense of continuity with the past while offering guidance and direction for the future (Elkind, 1998). What is different are the new social circumstances that require fresh adaptations. Put simply, the cosmopolitan adolescent is now perceived as sophisticated, as knowledgeable in matters of sex, drugs, technology and media. As with children, the perception of sophistication covers adaptational exchanges, replacements and innovations.

The Exchange of Sexual Values

Of the many social values that were exchanged during the turbulent decades of the 1960s and 1970s, the sexual were among the most prominent. Up until mid-century, pre-marital sex was socially unacceptable. To be sure, pre-marital sex was not unknown but it was socially frowned upon, even for engaged couples. All of that changed with the sexual revolution of the 1960s. It was brought about by a number of events — the introduction of effective birth control, the women's movement and the publication of research that demonstrated that women are as sexually responsive, or more so, than men. In the 1960s, pre-marital sex became socially acceptable and was celebrated in magazines, movies and television series.

Adolescents follow the adult model. When adults did not engage in pre-marital sex, at least openly and in large numbers, only a relatively small proportion of adolescents were sexually active. Once single adults were portrayed as sexually active in the media, adolescents were given a new sexual standard and a new sexual licence. The results were dramatic. Whereas as late as the 1960s only about 10 per cent of adolescent girls and 25 per cent of adolescent boys were sexually active, the figures are much higher today. According to centres for disease control, more than 50 per cent of twelfth-grade students report that they have had sexual intercourse and from the tenth grade on, the percentage of girls who report that they are sexually active is slightly higher than the percentage of boys (CFDCA, 1997).

In this case we have a clear example of how the larger society exchanged one value — pre-marital chastity — for another — pre-marital sexual activity. The adolescent generation exchanged its sexual values as well. One consequence was, until recently, an increase in teenage pregnancy and an explosive rise in the numbers of adolescents infected with sexually transmitted diseases. The exchange of sexual values has been maladaptive for many contemporary adolescents.

VANISHING SOCIETAL MARKERS AND THE APPEARANCE OF PEER GROUP MARKERS

In addition to an exchange of values, there has been a subtraction of markers. Markers are the signposts that we need as evidence of, in Kierkegaard's lovely phrase, our 'progress along life's way'. Markers give us a sense of where we stand both with respect to our own development and in relation to our peers. Although markers of development were commonplace in the late modern era, they have largely been subtracted from the lives of cosmopolitan children and adolescents. Yet young people, no less than adults, need markers to assess their changing personal and social status.

There were plenty of markers for provincial children and adolescents. Early in the twentieth century, to illustrate, children were dressed differently than were adults. Boys wore short trousers and getting into long pants was a rite of passage that was not permitted until early adolescence. Girls in turn were not allowed to wear make-up until they reached the teen years. Organised team sports were reserved for high school students, while children engaged in their own culture of childhood. Likewise, much information — about the family's financial affairs and family skeletons, for example — was deemed inappropriate for young ears. When young people were finally able to wear adult clothing, to engage in adult sports and be privy to adult information, they had clear evidence of their new social position. They had a clear sense that they had advanced to another stage along life's way.

Unfortunately, the cosmopolitan egalitarian ethos was inappropriately extended to children and youth. To treat children and adolescents as less than equal came to be regarded as condescending and a denial of their rights. As a result, many markers of child and adolescent development were simply eliminated. Even preschoolers now wear designer clothes, and make-up kits for girls aged from five to seven are no longer toys, but the real articles. From a distance it is difficult to tell an elementary school child from an adolescent. Activity markers have been eliminated as well. In many communities children as young as four or five are already in soccer clubs that travel away for games. In some communities, children as young as ten years old go out on dates. Cliques and clubs, once common only among adolescents, are now found among second and third graders. Information is no longer a marker either. In bookstores, one can find many books on homosexuality, AIDS, abuse, death and divorce written for young children.

Many of the markers that adolescents once used to distinguish themselves from children and to signal their transition to adulthood have thus been eliminated. Young people have been forced to replace these socially defined markers with their own, peer group-originated, symbols. One of these markers is rock groups. In the late modern era, rock music was used by adolescents to keep adults at bay. Today, it provides markers of development. Young adolescents follow some groups while older age groups follow others. Older adolescents, for example, would not be caught listening to the Back Street Boys, Britney Spears or the Spice Girls, favoured by younger adolescents. New music groups are generated at a rapid pace to give each new generation their own marker.

Other adaptations are not so much reflective of new accommodations as they are resurrections of earlier practices put to marker purposes. Body piercing and ornamentation are a case in point. Body piercing and tattooing have been practised at least as long as recorded history. They have, however, been resurrected by contemporary adolescents in most western societies. There are three usual explanations for choosing these new marker symbols. One explanation is associated with the need for individual expression of the self in the postmodern, mass-market age. From this point of view, body ornamentation gives the individual control over at least part of the self that has been wrested away by a global consumer economy that dictates what young people want and need. A second explanation is that body ornamentation is a means of social protest. It is a way of showing adult society that young people are in charge of their own destiny and are able to make long-term decisions, such as having and maintaining a tattoo. A third explanation sees body ornamentation as simply a passing adolescent fad, no different in many respects from bobby socks and penny loafers of an earlier generation. In many ways these fads are copied from the rock stars of the moment.

These explanations are not mutually exclusive and may all have some validity. My own explanation is related, but a bit different. Although society has subtracted many markers from children and adolescents, young people still need them. I believe that, in part at least, body piercing and ornamentation serve as markers for a special status. Nose rings, green hair, and tattoos are markers. Body ornamentation separates adolescents from children who may want to wear such markers but are prohibited from doing so. But it also separates them from, at least, most adults. Moreover, they can be given up, perhaps with the exception of tattoos, once young people reach maturity. This marker explanation does not gainsay the others, but does point to the adaptive value of this practice. Young people, if not adults, often regard these new markers as supporting the perception of adolescent sophistication.

Technological Innovation and New Talents

The third adaptational shift supporting the perception of sophistication has been mediated by the new technologies. These technologies have helped many adolescents to develop potentials that, at other times in history, might never have been realised. The aptitude many young people have for technology, particularly computers, often surpasses that of adults. Many teenagers, for example, now do all the computer work for their parents, set up web pages, and even handle the family's finances and investments on the Internet.

While the realisation of these new talents contributes to young people's feelings of self-confidence and esteem, it can have its dark side. While their computer skills may put them on a par with adults, they are still young. Those who work with them may not appreciate their continuing need for adult guidance and moral leadership. And their ready access to the web also makes them the target of those who sell pornography or who wish to get them to gamble on line. Nonetheless, the information age has unleashed adolescent talents, never seen before, that are uniquely suited to the demands of an information age.

CONCLUSION

In this essay, I have suggested that the family can be viewed as a social organism that must adapt to the demands of its social habitat. When society changes so too must the family. I have described the changes that families made in values, roles and perceptions to adapt to the movement from a modern to a postmodern society. I have suggested that the modern nuclear family was an adaptation to the demands of industrial society, while the cosmopolitan family is an adaptation to the demands of the postmodern world. I have also suggested that nuclear family adaptation was better suited to the needs of children and youth than it was to the needs of parents. In contrast, the adaptations of the cosmopolitan family seem better suited to the needs of parents than they are to the needs of their offspring.

We are, however, still in a transitional period when the selection of the most adaptive family forms is still in play. One can only hope that the outcome will be a *vital* family whose values, roles and perceptions will meet the needs of both parents and children while bringing them into equilibrium with the demands of the social habitat.

References

Bernard, J. (1981). 'The good provider role: Its rise and fall' in *American Psychologist*, Vol. 36, No. 1, pp. 1-12.

CFDCA (1997). *Youth Risk Behaviour Surveillance*. Atlanta: Centre for Disease Control.

Elkind, D. (1998). *All Grown Up and No Place to Go*. Reading MA: Perseus.

Gesell, A. and F.L. Illg (1943). *Infant and Child in the Culture of Today*. New York: Harper.

Matthews, G. (1987). *Just a Housewife*. New York. Oxford University Press.

Parsons, T. (1951). *The Social System*. Glencoe, Ill: The Free Press.

Spock, B. (1976). *Baby and Child Care*. New York: Hawthorne.

Winnicott, D. (1987). *Babies and Mothers*. Reading, MA: Addison-Wesley.

Chapter 4

SUFFER LITTLE CHILDREN?
THE HISTORICAL VALIDITY OF
MEMOIRS OF IRISH CHILDHOOD

Diarmaid Ferriter

I

In a perceptive review article published by the *Sunday Tribune* in June 2000, archivist and critic Catriona Crowe sought to make sense of the seemingly insatiable appetite in Ireland and beyond for memoirs of Irish childhood. She noted that

> the whole business of untold stories is at the heart of our fascination with these revelations. The private domain of personal experience has always been at odds with the official stories which were sanctioned, permitted and encouraged by the state and the Catholic Church.

Developing this theme, Crowe suggested

> these memoirs run like a parallel stream of information alongside the official documentary record and complement it with their personal immediacy and vibrancy. The official

record can tell us what happened, but rarely what it felt
like (*Sunday Tribune*, 18 June 2000).

Crowe's conclusions highlight the importance of a genre of writing that has done much to expose what might be defined as the
'underbelly' of Irish state and society at a crucial time in the development of modern Ireland. Much of the testimony is bleak, and
at times harrowing, and it is strongly tempting to conclude from
an engagement with these texts that the greatest blot on twentieth-century Irish society's copybook was its treatment of children.
Their value lies not only in the articulation of personal experience,
but also the light they shed on key themes of modern Irish history. Whether or not they are representative of the generality of
Irish childhood experience is a more difficult question to answer.
As Frank McCourt pointed out in the first page of *Angela's Ashes*,
'the happy childhood is hardly worth your while' (McCourt, 1996,
p. 1). With some notable exceptions, publishers and writers seem
to agree.

One of the purposes memoirs of Irish childhood fulfil is to
highlight the huge gulf that existed between the rhetoric of aspiration that coloured so many of the expressions of Ireland's supposed advantages as an unsullied rural idyll, firmly grounded on
the institution of the family, and the reality of a society, and indeed of many families, that failed hopelessly to live up to such
rhetoric. An important component of the Irish cultural revival in
the early twentieth century, identified by Declan Kiberd, involved
the idealisation of Irish childhood. As a reaction to Ireland's colonial status, it seemed childhood, like Ireland itself, had to be recreated as a place of innocence, unsullied by contamination or
complication, to reinforce the nationalist claim that Ireland un-
governed by an external agent would be a purer Ireland. The focus in literary texts was not on what childhood was or is; rather,
the child became 'an expendable cultural object . . . based on the
widespread but false assumption that childhood exists outside of
the culture in which it is produced as a state of unspoilt nature'
(Kiberd, 1995, p. 311). Many of the memoirs appertaining to

childhood in pre- and post-independent Ireland expose this for the fallacy it was.

It is ironic that most memoirs of childhood describe the experience of growing up in what many believed was a century in which the concept of 'children's rights' was esteemed, and indeed, vigorously promoted. Commenting on the introduction of extremely limited legal adoption in Ireland in 1952, Liam Maher observed contentedly in the Catholic periodical *Irish Monthly*, that

> there has been a growing interest in the plight of homeless and unwanted children as the social conscience has become more sensitive towards the unprotected and the underprivileged. This has been called the century of the child (Wyley, 1992).

Given the emphasis placed on the family in public discourse, it may have been thought that Irish society was particularly conscious of its responsibilities in this regard. G.K. Chesterton famously remarked that 'wherever there is Ireland there is the family and it counts for a great deal' (Kiberd, 1995, p. 313). Disturbingly, many of the memoirs reveal that the institution of the family often masked the calculated savagery that was a feature of the treatment afforded children. Moreover, the state hardly performed better as many children taken away from what were identified as ailing or failing families experienced brutality and harshness in institutions funded and protected by the state that effectively deprived them of what can be defined as childhood.

The desire to improve the manner in which children were treated was a prominent feature of the rhetoric of the Irish revolution (1918–23), as the rebels piously promised they would make amends for the harshness of their Victorian oppressors. But many of the actual opinions of this revolutionary generation were incompatible with such aspirations. W.T. Cosgrave, Minister for Local Government during the period of the revolution, certainly held out few expectations for the children pining in the workhouses that Sinn Féin was dedicated to abolishing. Writing privately to the Minister for Home Affairs, he maintained in May 1921 that:

> People reared in workhouses, as you are aware, are no great acquisition to the community and they have no ideas whatever of civic responsibilities. As a rule their highest aim is to live at the expense of the ratepayers. Consequently, it would be a decided gain if they all took it into their heads to emigrate. When they go abroad they are thrown on their own responsibilities and have to work whether they like it or not (National Archives of Ireland, DE 2/84, 3 May 1921).

Eamon de Valera's most quoted broadcast — the 1943 St Patrick's day 'Ireland that we dreamed of' speech — is often perceived as an articulation of a hopelessly unreal and romanticised vision of rural existence. Its reference to 'cosy homesteads' and the 'laughter of comely maidens', in particular, have been singled out for aspersion by a generation who paid the price when de Valera's society failed to allow them live in comfort in Ireland. Joe Lee has recently suggested that this speech was important because of the emphasis it attached to the links between generations and the dependent ages in society — childhood, youth and old age — and because it stressed that rights in Irish society had to be balanced by responsibilities. Yet, on any reading of the speech in the light of the revelations of the last decade, the phrase 'the romping of sturdy children' stands out in ironic counterpoint to official image and aspiration. Many, we now know, were failed by the precious contract between the dependent generations; many, we now know, had no recognised rights; many, we now know, were burdened with responsibilities which should not have been theirs. There are few children romping sturdily in the books under consideration here.

II

Over 40 titles have been consulted in the preparation of this essay. They span the century and vary greatly in length, detail, style and content, in common with the class and background of their authors. The books are diverse and subjective. In order to deal with such a range, a thematic framework is best employed to highlight consistencies and inconsistencies within these recorded experiences and to suggest how they may be fitted into a more historical context. To this end, the following themes have been chosen on the basis that they are the issues which dominate most of the texts under review — societal background; mothers and fathers; violence and abuse; happiness; death; religion and class. It also has to be stressed that for all the examples given there are countless others that could be cited to reinforce the arguments put forward, and that these categories are by no means exclusive.

Despite the well-publicised controversies over what constitutes accurate memory, we should not be under any illusion that the exposure of bleak Irish childhoods began in 1996 with the publication of the phenomenally successful *Angela's Ashes* by Frank McCourt. This searing, provocative and challenging account of childhood poverty deserves its seven million readers, not because it is about growing up in Limerick but because it describes impoverished childhood in a powerful and vivid manner. It deals with a universal theme, and is written through the eyes of a child, which is why it gained a universal audience. But one can find many earlier accounts of marginalised children. One of the earliest is Patrick McGill's *Children of the Dead*. Published in 1914, it deals with a bleak childhood in Edwardian Donegal. Like thousands of other youngsters, McGill was brought to a hiring fair at the age of 12. His depiction of the fairs and his subsequent treatment at the hands of rapacious employers is encapsulated in the observation:

> To him I was not a human being, a boy with an appetite and a soul. I was merely a ware purchased in the market place, something of less value than a plough and of no more account than a barrow.

The money he earned as a result of his labour was sent home, and McGill's reflections on this cruel economy are equally revealing about parental attitudes to children in families struggling for basic subsistence:

> I was born and bred merely to support my parents and great care had been taken to drive this fact into my mind from infancy. I was merely brought into the world to support those who were responsible for my existence (McGill, 1914, pp. 36–7).

Yet McGill was born during an era when children were beginning to be noticed as individuals susceptible to neglect and ill-treatment. Legislatively and officially, the late nineteenth century witnessed an important shift in attitude in this respect, a development symbolised by the formation in 1889 in Dublin of the Society for the Prevention of Cruelty to Children. Eimear Burke has noted that the 1880s onwards signalled the legitimisation of the 'normal' child within the family, in contrast to previous practice when attention was focused more on deserted, illegitimate and orphaned children. Members of Dublin Corporation and societies such as the DSPCC and the Women's National Health Association sought to implement public health and welfare schemes for mothers, infants and children, and did improve the lot of many, though they were also resented by some as interfering upper and middle-class philanthropists. Furthermore, as Burke observes, one of the arguments used by those opposed to the establishment of the DSPCC was to repudiate the claim that Dublin children were maltreated. It was even suggested that to admit the existence of cruelty would destroy the image of Ireland as the 'maternal isle' (Burke, 1990, p. 111). The courts did not sustain this image, but given that just over 300 people were charged with neglect of children in 1900 and only 150 in 1918, it did not seem a major problem. While the Children's Act of 1908 was regarded as a fundamental step in extending child protection, incorporating in one statute a host of amending laws and piecemeal legislation which emphasised the social rights of children, it was in practice more parent-centred (in the sense of bringing them to account for neglect) than child-centred. Crucially, it also directed that 'the courts should be agencies for the rescue as well as the punishment of children' (Wyley, 1992, p. 19). It was this Act that provided the legal basis for the state's engagement with the problems of child welfare in Ireland for most of the twentieth century.

Ultimately, the institutional option was favoured. Between 1858 and 1969, 15,899 children were committed to reformatory schools; and between 1869 and 1969, 105,000 Irish children were committed to industrial schools (O'Sullivan and Raftery, 1999, p. 52). From the beginning, the welfare record of these institutions was shameful; between 1869 and 1913, 48,664 children were admitted to industrial schools of whom 2,623 (5.39 per cent) died while in custody. There was nothing uniquely Irish about the system of institutionalisation, but ultimately the crucial difference in Ireland's approach was that at a time when Britain saw the defects in this system and sought reform (industrial schools were abolished in the United Kingdom in 1933), the Irish authorities clung relentlessly to the system. As Mary Raftery and Eoin O'Sullivan point out in *Suffer the Little Children*:

> The newly independent Ireland took the opposite course, opting for the interlocking system of industrial, reformatory and Magdalen. Instead of addressing poverty, neglect and class division it funded religious orders to effectively incarcerate these children. This use of child care by the religious orders to methodically entrench and perpetuate a rigid class system in Ireland remains one of the most hidden aspects of these structures (O'Sullivan and Raftery, 1999, p. 69).

By 1924 there were more children in industrial schools in the Free State than there were in all of the industrial schools in England, Scotland, Wales and Northern Ireland put together. It should also be noted that many lower down the social scale experienced no better care in the old County Homes.

III

How was this process of institutionalisation perceived by the children of independent Ireland who have recorded their experiences? In the context of the courts which, as mentioned above, were agencies of rescue as well as punishment, there was a perception of exclusion and powerlessness. Mary Norris from Killarney, an interviewee in *Suffer the Little Children*, recalled:

> [T]hey took us out and up to the village where there was a court. We were like sheep going to a fair, to a slaughter. We all stood there in front of this judge and he put us away (O'Sullivan and Raftery, 1999, p. 69).

Paddy Doyle, brought to Wexford District Court in 1955 after the suicide of his father, and too young to understand the process, recalled in *The God Squad* that 'reading a journalist's report of that event made me realise that this was not a secret, unheard of event, but a public domain issue' (Doyle, 1988, p. 10). Mannix Flynn, author of *Nothing to Say*, an account of his experiences in Letterfrack industrial school, articulated the harrowing guilt and reality that lay behind clinical press reports about a court routine with which he was becoming increasingly familiar. The guilt was not for his petty crimes, but his mother, realising it was she who would suffer the most, along with the countless other mothers who smoked nervously in waiting rooms:

> Everything inside me began to hate this oul cunt of a judge. I felt like lifting the clock off the mantelpiece and fucking it at her. To me she was a cold bastard. My mother was crying, weeping, asking the judge for another chance (Flynn, 1983, p. 38).

It seems also that little changed in the reports of the probation officers as they detailed the all too familiar tales of drink, housing, marriage and schooling problems. In an insightful indictment of a system that sought to remove rather than repair, Flynn observes: 'and on it went, the same old story, the classical cliché: I could never understand these reports'. Was it a question of 'study the report and find the answer' or was it a question of 'get a report and find the problem'? Bernadette Fahey, sent to Goldenbridge orphanage, recalled the cruelty of the courtroom, for many children their first introduction to adult environments, and wondered if judges realised the implications of their decisions (Fahey, 1999, p. 52). Perhaps one of the cruellest aspects of some judges' decisions was their determination to place children at as far a remove from their home as possible, thereby putting even more distance between them and their parents.

It is difficult to escape the image of the bereft mother in these memoirs. Throughout many of the testimonies the mothers emerge as extraordinary individuals in ordinary and sometimes desperate surroundings. Mannix Flynn's mother embraced the task undertaken by many, not just of rearing her own children, but also her grandchildren. Recalling his sister's pregnancy, Flynn wrote:

> I remember the time she got pregnant. The house was in uproar; the shame of it, the pain of it and what in the name of Jazus are we going to do about it? My mother kept the child and reared it (Flynn, 1983, p. 30).

Did any of these women reach their full potential? Peter Sheridan in his memoir of life in Dublin's Sheriff Street observed his mother 'at all times being careful. Being less than who she was. I watched her do all this because it wasn't safe for her to do anything else' (Sheridan, 1999, p. 144). Molly Baines, the mother in Paul Smith's *The Countrywoman* (bravely published in 1962 and set in 1920s slum Dublin) is burdened with a violent and abusive monster of a husband and has continually to negotiate the pendulum of his moods and the tangibility of his anger. To this end, she developed the skill of:

> . . . listening to the sounds his voice made without hearing what he said. She could gauge instantly the extent of his wrath and, when he was sober, whether or not to expect

> violence, by the near shading of the rise and fall of a sound that alerted her and put her on her guard (Smith, 1962, p. 115).

Depictions of struggling, though resourceful, women are commonplace; but the memoirs of those who had the luxury of wealth and social position are also revealing of the trials women endured. Marriage was not an institution in which women flourished. Novelist Kathleen Coyle, growing up in comfort in Derry at the turn of the century, recalled the glow in her home environment which was created by her mother, perhaps to offset the effect of her father's drinking and volatility. From the scraps of conversation she heard as a child, she noted that verdicts always depended upon what men were and what women were not. Women were talked about in negative terms; judgements were cast upon them in darkness, never in the light: 'It was what was said in a whisper'. Women were controlled by marriage in a way in which men were not controlled:

> Our marriages, grandmother bewailed often, and always wrung her hands. All of them seemed to have married without approval or against their will (Coyle, 1943, p. 196).

Nuala O'Faoláin's mother, who had to cope with thirteen pregnancies, is depicted harshly as not wanting

> anything to do with child-rearing or housework. But she had to do it. Because she fell in love with my father and they married, she was condemned to spend her life as a mother and a homemaker. She was in the wrong job (O'Faoláin, 1996, p. 14).

Significantly, children who lost mothers when still very young were not encouraged in many households to reflect on their loss, to deal with their grief or communicate their resultant fears. Seán Dunne, in his memoir of growing up in Waterford in the 1960s, remembered that after his mother died at the age of 33, when he was four years old, he latched on to whatever scraps he could:

> [T]o hear someone talk of my mother could give me thoughts for days. Yet my mother's family seemed a family of ghosts, of lives spent with suffering and drawn into death when young (Dunne, 1991, p. 68).

Edith Newman Devlin, reared in a stern Protestant house in the grounds of Swift's Hospital in Dublin city, was never allowed deal with the loss of her mother who succumbed to cancer. She wrote that 'after her death, no one spoke of her again. The word mammy was never again heard in our house.' Her father, who lived until he was 85, would not mention his wife's name, and she recorded bitterly that 'unwittingly he had dammed up my natural feelings and by impoverishing my early memories had weakened me for the very future he was preparing me for' (Devlin, 2000, pp. 39–45). She replaced her mother with books.

Mothers coping alone could also be judged harshly, though they often endured squalor that was emotional as much as physical. Robert Harbinson, writing in 1960 of his Ulster childhood, dedicated his work to his mother, 'Big Ina', a young widow who laboured fourteen hours a day, seven days a week as a charwoman to ensure her children would not see the inside of an orphanage, 'and often we were her worst enemies. We stole from her and wrecked the home she tried to keep for us'. And yet, in the eyes of the child who emotionally needed more than could be given in such sparse environments, it was still the mother who ultimately would be judged, as witnessed in the starkness of Harbinson's line: 'In all the years of my childhood, I cannot remember my mother embracing me' (Harbinson, 1960, p. 55).

But what of these women's own childhoods? Hadn't many of them too been deprived of youth, of the ability to grow independently? Lily O'Connor, in her memoir of growing up as a Protestant in Dublin's tenement slums wrote simply:

> Down on her knees, scrubbing the floorboards in a tenement room, Mammy suddenly remembered it was her twenty-first birthday. She had been married two years and had two young children (O'Connor, 2000, p. 12).

Since many mothers were surrounded by death from a very early stage they were urged to see it as an essential part of mothering rather than an occasion for personalised reflection. At one stage, the most famous mother of all, Angela McCourt, insists after another harrowing death of a child: 'All I want now is a little peace, ease and comfort'. But it is another mother who shatters the illusion that respite is in any way possible or even desirable:

> Grandma comes and tells Mam she has to get up. There are children dead, she says, but there are children alive and they need their mother.

Despite the lengths she goes to provide succour, ultimately Angela too is judged harshly by her children — for trading her body for a roof and food for her children, and for begging. McCourt wrote: 'my mother is a beggar now and if anyone from the Lane or my school sees her the family will be disgraced entirely'. And, yet in the midst of all this, Angela's capacity to see poverty as relative is almost saintly: 'she says there are always people worse off' (McCourt, 1996, p. 250).

Motherhood in abject circumstances inevitably took its toll, physically and emotionally. John McGahern in *The Barracks* described his cancer-stricken stepmother attempting to deal with the painful realisation that the children will not see her as a second mother, even though she was not in a position to have children of her own. She knew Willie didn't trust her and wouldn't confide in her, despite the care and attention she lavished on the children, all the while negotiating the temperament of their bitter and bullying father. And what did she get in return? The hurtful phrase, 'didn't we manage for ages before you ever came?' (McGahern, 1963, p. 39).

The memoir record tells us that many mothers succumbed in face of the pressure to be good mothers at all costs. The demise of Molly Baines, Paul Smith's *Countrywoman*, is heart-wrenching. Smith's work is a searing indictment of the emotional and physical imprisonment of women. Yet the harrowing domestic scenes are matched by callous official disinterest. When hospital treatment is required, Molly is not only publicly humiliated but informed by the nurse 'of course a man isn't responsible for his actions in drink'. Having stretched all resources, been resilient, kind, and, as with many of these women, exceptionally resourceful, Molly is left to die alone in the County Home. Her son Tommy Tucker, a boy who still needs his mother but who cannot visit her, suddenly feels the desire to smash his father's face into sensibility:

> ... into regretting all the suddenly now vividly remembered vicious pains and anxieties that it had rained into his mother's life, and withered her into crippled ill-health and old age when she was still young (Smith, 1962, p. 325).

IV

A majority of fathers emerge from the published memoirs of childhood as utterly unlikeable, disreputable, drunken, and incapable of communication. Even Peter Sheridan's somewhat smug memoir of the child who idolises his father cannot conceal the fact that this was a man who, to the outsider, is a bully who commands, controls and sulks if proven incorrect. In the opening section the reader is treated to a recollection of his father's flatulence:

> Da let out a crisp beautiful fart. He whistled with satisfaction. The smell was awful but I liked it. It was amazing the stink he could make (Sheridan, 1999, p. 5).

Of course adulation by a young boy of his father is not untypical, and Sheridan, like many, comes to realise his father's flaws. Nonetheless, his endless description of his father performing mundane tasks is a laborious read and the manner in which Sheridan senior is incapable of admitting wrong only serves to reinforce pity for the mother. Moreover, Peter Sheridan's conclusion that 'Dad was a good person. He gave the world seven children' is trite, does scant justice to the complexities of parenting or the perception of children, and seems a gross injustice to mothers (Sheridan, 1999, p. 5).

The ability and determination of fathers to control the temperature of the domestic environment is a consistent feature of these memoirs of childhood, as is the degree to which they blamed others. Smith noted in the *Countrywoman* that 'as usual he considered that his wife and children were responsible for the tortures of his life' (Smith, 1962, p. 114). John McGahern refers to the fact that the father in his work *The Barracks* 'had an intense pity for himself and would fly into a passion of reproaches if he got any provocation' (McGahern, 1963, p. 42). Edith Devlin appreciated the circumstances in which her father was left alone with a young family. Maids became the focus of his bullying, with his desire to do his best for his children diminished by his inability to understand his children's feelings. In response, Edith withdraws and begins the long years of non-communication. He was a stranger whom she feared, a stranger whose presence was omnipotent:

> His swings of mood were so erratic that we never knew when the blow was going to fall and the only strategy we could develop against an unjust attack was to know at every moment of the day where we were physically, in relation to him. No mouse was ever more wary of the cat than we were of our father (Devlin, 2000, p. 87).

Malachy McCourt in *Angela's Ashes* seems consistently to find solace in the past because of his inability to navigate the present. Frank observed that his father was like the Holy Trinity, with three people within him — the avid newspaper reader and Republican who lapped up politics past and present; the great storyteller who thrived on entertaining his children; and the feckless drunk who drank the money sent for a newborn baby, a man 'gone beyond the beyonds as my mother would say' (McCourt, 1996, p. 186). Nuala O'Faoláin, alluding to her father's cruel, violent and drunken streak, noted that although he contributed little to their upbringing, he still managed to have an all-pervasive presence.

Memoirs of upper-class life are also revealing of the emotional distance that separated fathers and their children. Enid Starkie's *A*

Lady's Child, published in 1949, recounts a materially privileged upbringing; her father was a classics scholar and the last resident commissioner of education for Ireland under British rule. She noted that as a child they lived a life of Victorian ease and plenty; that her father held for her a great glamour, but that 'I was too much in awe of him to get to know him thoroughly' (Starkie, 1949, p. 12). He, she wrote, 'only knew us with our party manners' and 'though I loved and admired him more than anything else in my life, I could not have told him of the dark dreams that filled my mind; of the anxieties which I did not myself understand' (Starkie, 1949, p. 212). Starkie went on to become an internationally renowned expert on French literature. As her biographer noted, she could play the intellectual bohemian or the Grande Dame, the Irish waif or the exotic hostess (Richardson, 1973). Such celebrated eccentricity, however, may have masked what was in reality loneliness — she wanted more than her orthodox Edwardian parents could give her and craved an uncritical love, which she had missed in childhood. Like others from privileged backgrounds, she found solace in literature.

An exception to the distant father stereotype is found in Dermot Healy's tender and warm relationship with his father in *The Bend for Home*. Healy writes unashamedly that he and his bed-ridden father 'grew so close it was painful', as he sat by his father's bedside for two years with his books propped against his knees (Healy, 1996, pp. 103ff). Maurice O'Sullivan, in *Twenty Years a Growing*, dealing with his childhood on the Blasket Islands, is another who grew up without his mother, but her loss was not hugely felt, partly because he had a father who allowed him to experience the freedom of his environment, which in itself nurtured, developed and protected him (O'Sullivan, 1953).

V

It was an unfortunate reality for some that childhood was synonymous with violence and abuse, physical and sexual. Collectively, these memoirs emphatically underline the danger many children experienced on a regular basis. Much publicity has been given in recent years to the extent of abuse and the measures taken to cover it up, but what is significant from the published memoirs of childhood is the different ways in which it is depicted. Perhaps this is where the value of human testimony, when placed alongside the official record, is at its most powerful. The scale of violence and abuse was not acknowledged publicly or officially; occasional leaks of information, and the reaction to them, reveal a state and society that was determined, almost ruthlessly, to deny it. The extent to which heinous abuse could be systematically inflicted within the family over an extended period was bravely articulated in *Sophia's Story*, published in 1998 (McKay, 1998). Had the book been published ten years previously it is doubtful if it would have been afforded the same credibility. In that year, 1988, Paddy Doyle received a more sceptical reaction to his story of, amongst other things, the violence employed by the nuns of St Michael's Industrial School in Cappaquinn. He recalled:

> I used to hear people refer to me as one of the children from the orphanage, which was the phrase locals used to soften the brutal reality of the industrial school in their midst (Doyle, 1988, p. 38).

That brutality also involved sexual abuse, though this issue was not acknowledged in Irish society during Doyle's childhood. Significantly, the Carrigan Report of 1931 that highlighted the way judicial processes operated to the detriment of children was suppressed, though in the course of its preparation evidence was heard from Garda Commissioner, Eoin O'Duffy, of an alarming increase in sexual crime and paedophilia 'with girls . . . from 16 years downwards including many cases of children under ten years' (Kennedy, 2000, p. 328). Less than 15 per cent of these cases were prosecuted. Moreover, the Minister for Justice, James Geoghegan, deemed this appropriate since he held that such claims were wildly exaggerated. More revealingly, he did not rate the evidence of children, noting, 'a child with a vivid imagination may actually live in his mind the situation as he invented it and will be quite unshaken by severe cross-examination'. Finola Kennedy correctly points out that the suppression of the Carrigan Report ensured a continuation of ignorance and lack of debate about child abuse, as the government chose to deny any evidence of moral impropriety in the fledgling Free State (Kennedy, 2000).

The reports of the National Society for the Prevention of Cruelty to Children from the 1940s and 1950s provided evidence to sustain this conclusion. In the year 1944–45, the society dealt with 1,103 cases, the overwhelming majority classed under the heading 'neglect'. No cases were listed under the headings 'criminal and indecent assault'. Only eighteen people were prosecuted, and the report indicated that 'of real and deliberate cruelty to children there has been practically none' (NSPCC, 1944–45). This was representative of the general tone of the reports mid-century. Nonetheless, there were grounds for concern as NSPCC reports detailing specific cases of neglect, squalor and parental irresponsibility sustained their case for legal adoption, and their strong criticism of the excessive use of industrial schools as an alternative to providing a new family life for the victims. Yet, in 1956, when Archbishop McQuaid assumed control of the Society, the challenging and graphic case studies were omitted; the awkward questions posed about adoption and industrial schools were replaced with quaint and superficial stories with happy endings. There was no context and no challenge. The exposure of the underbelly ceased and the Society's aim remained essentially conservative, focused on damage limitation —'the primary function of our Society is to ensure that the life of every child in the state shall at least be endurable' (NSPCC, 1963–68).

Yet worrying evidence of abuse and neglect was not difficult to find. Anna McCabe, the Medical Inspector of the Industrial Schools, described in her reports conditions of near starvation, and of their being 'no human interest whatsoever in the children' (NSPCC, 1963–68, pp. 120ff). Some of her reports were akin to those written by workhouse inspectors during the Great Famine. They were not acted on. The probability is that these schools could literally kill children. The sealing up of a well at Baltimore

Industrial School, County Cork (a well which had been used to punish children by making them cling to its inside), and the coinciding disappearance of a child, speaks volumes about what probably happened when punishment went too far (O'Sullivan and Raftery, 1999, p. 147). It is significant also that the most glaring omissions from the archives dealing with Industrial Schools is information on the deaths of children.

A fascinating exchange in the Dáil in April 1954 is revealing of the mindset that refused to recognise the problem of abuse. This arose from a query raised by Dublin TD Peadar Cowan, following a call from a constituent, the mother of an inmate of Artane industrial school. She had been refused permission to see her son, in hospital after a 21-year-old Christian Brother had viciously beaten him with a sweeping brush. Cowan prefaced his query by waxing lyrical about Artane and the Brothers (it was not until 1960 that he bravely acknowledged institutionalised sex abuse (Cowan, 1960)). But he did want an assurance that punishment would be inflicted by persons of experience and responsibility. Significantly, the minister responsible, Sean Moylan, did not deny that the incident had taken place. Rather, he sought to downplay it as an 'accident', and to exonerate the Christian Brothers of any wrongdoing:

> I cannot conceive any deliberate ill treatment of boys by a community motivated by the ideals of its founder. I cannot conceive any sadism emanating from men who were trained to have devotion to a very high purpose. The point is that accidents happen in the best-regulated families and in this family there are about 800 boys. These boys are difficult to control. At times maybe it is essential that children should be punished. This is an isolated incident; it can only happen again as an accident. . . . I would point out to parents that any guarantee I give them of full protection of their children is no licence to any of the children to do what they like (*Dáil Debates*, 23 April 1954).

In subsequent decades, others sought to ensure a change in the legal status of children, especially in the context of adoption, guardianship and orphanage, notably Charles Haughey, who in the 1960s and 1970s was zealous in his efforts to champion the cause of vulnerable children. The Tuairim Report of 1966 drew attention to inadequacies in the residential care of deprived children that ultimately led to the Kennedy Report on industrial schools, which marked the beginning of the end of the industrial school regime. During the 1970s and 1980s, socially conscious middle-class campaigners like Alan Shatter and Mary Robinson championed the cause of children and achieved some success, though governments, even in the 1980s, would not abolish the concept of illegitimacy. The Children's Act of 1908 also remained stubbornly on the statute books (McGearty, 1995).

VI

The memoirs of childhood published in the last two decades are particularly revealing of what it felt like to be an abuse victim. The recurring theme is fear. The amount of fear packed into the first six years of Paddy Doyle's life almost defies belief, which was why darkness 'came as a blessing, a place of refuge'; which was why urinating on himself created 'a warm pleasurable feeling' that he did not get from anywhere else (Doyle, 1988, p. 23). It was for the same reasons that the only respite he got from abuse was when he became ill and hospitalised, which is another recurring theme in many of these stories. Abuse simply had to be got used to, according to Mannix Flynn:

> Everything that I owned was being taken away from me piece by piece and was being replaced by something. That something I couldn't figure out, so I could not fight it or protect myself against it. I felt there was nothing I could do about it except get used to it.

The violence was in turn mirrored in the behaviour of some of the boys. The tenderness of Flynn's initial sexual encounter with another boy in the laundry room gave way to fear when he was sexually abused by an older boy (Flynn, 1983, pp. 63, 114). Bernadette Fahey not only recalls the ritual public humiliation of punishment, but also how she too became capable of cruelty (Fahey, 1999, p. 122). For Seán Maher, in his memoirs as a travelling child, fighting was an intrinsic part of being a traveller and 'in the end the child can only continue as his parents did before him'. 'A punch now and again does us no harm', his mother informed him (Maher, 1972, p. 19).

Many of those at school were accustomed to, if not casual about, abuse. Seán Dunne recalls a teacher offering a boy a choice of the weapons with which he would be beaten (Dunne, 1991, p. 43). Edith Devlin recalled a favourite rhyme in her Dublin city neighbourhood:

> Mr Kelly is a very good man, he goes to church on Sunday,
> and prays to God to give him strength to wallop the boys
> on Monday (Devlin, 2000, p. 69).

For Dermot Healy, 'when you stepped into Brother Felim's class with the roll-call book he brought you in behind his desk and felt your mickey as you called out the names' (Healy, 1996, p. 102). Barney, an interviewee in *Suffer the Little Children*, revealed of an abuser that 'he didn't even have the goodness to bugger you in private' (O'Sullivan and Raftery, 1999, p. 273).

In contrast, Gene Kerrigan's account of growing up in 1950s Dublin is that of a happy childhood, and intermittent classroom violence did not mitigate this contentment:

> Mr McAuliffe didn't hit us more often than the average observer of that time might have considered necessary. It didn't change our view of him. He was still a nice man, a man who liked children. Hitting us was just something that adults were supposed to do.

He also recalled that the revelations which dominated the 1990s were 'as alien to us as the dark side of the moon, we who were living through the best years of our lives' (Kerrigan, 1998, pp. 38–9).

VII

Kerrigan's observations remind us that not all memoirs of Irish childhood are negative. There have been many commercially successful accounts that describe growing up in seemingly idyllic circumstances in independent Ireland, which must be taken into account even when they are syrupy and devoid of a wider context. Significantly, Kerrigan's does not fit this category, as his perceptive observation that 'we weren't conscious of the moulding process, of the limitations hemming us in, the insistence on guilt and deference' emphasises (Kerrigan, 1998, p. 26). Kerrigan, in short, warns against transposing adult realisations onto childhood experience 'where pure happiness came instantly and unalloyed' (Kerrigan, 1998, p. 122). Maurice O'Sullivan's *Twenty Years a Growing* provides another illustration of this. As he negotiates each new experience growing up on the Blasket Islands, one of O'Sullivan's recurrent phrases is 'the delight in my heart was growing' (O'Sullivan, 1953, p. 125). These observations are placed in the context of children negotiating an adult world, but it is one that allowed children to learn from their own mistakes and that equipped them with the language to express their growing experience with insight. In many ways O'Sullivan's memoir chronicles an upbringing that is the exact opposite of institutionalisation, but is revealing of the benefits that accrue when children are free to roam and to express themselves freely, with guidance and supervision from those who have been exposed to the realities of living openly, often dangerously, but ultimately independently.

As for other happy memoirs, Catriona Crowe has observed that it was hard to believe that so many children's lives could have been damaged in the most fundamental way in a country in which Alice Taylor's *To School through the Fields*, a best-selling memoir about an idyllic childhood in County Cork in the 1940s, was perceived to reflect normative experience (*Sunday Tribune*, 18 June 2000). The problem for the critic with a work such as this is that it is memoir as fantasy rather than as a contribution to social history. All the memoirs of bleak childhoods are notable for their recollection of what made them happy, what gave them pleasure and relief, as well as what damaged them. For all the monsters and abusers there are always appearances, however brief and fleeting, of saints and saviours, whom the children remember vividly and fondly. With the idyllic memoirs, however, there is not a hint of darkness. This is not to deny Taylor's experience or others similar to it, but to question the complete absence of any significant wider context, or any allusion to the challenges of rural existence. Lisnasheoga, Taylor's home place, is possessed of a fairy-tale quality: 'We were free to be children and to grow up at our own pace in a quiet place close to the earth', she writes. All the animals live in peaceful bliss; friends have 'perfect understanding', and faith in the goodness of human nature means one can 'live to a ripe old age and still believe that this is a wonderful world and everybody in it is as good as they can be' (Taylor, 1988, p. 47 ff).

Taylor writes about 'rare moments of perfection', seemingly oblivious to the fact that rare implies seldom, whereas her memory deems perfection to have been ubiquitous. Rory O'Connor's recent *Gander at the Gate*, articulating an idyllic Kerry childhood, is in the same league; as a small child, O'Connor 'had a feeling that there was magic and mystery everywhere, that I lived in a special place'. He writes lovingly of a heavenly, angelic mother; of farm-yards of wonder; and of complete perfection in terms of the environment. A typical passage from O'Connor reads:

> Primroses, cowslips, buttercups, violets and bluebells called on me to look at them as they moved in the light morning breeze. The sun was warm on my bare feet and the golden brown dust of the road crept into the small spaces between my toes (O'Connor, 2000, p. 55 ff).

Does childhood awe really manifest itself in observations of this kind, or is it a case of adult perception and appreciation of nature being artificially placed in the mind of the child?

VIII

Rory O'Connor noted that 'in the early few years I thought none of us would ever die' (O'Connor, 2000, p. 94). Unfortunately, this was not the experience of most of these memoirists to whom death appeared regularly. This is not surprising of a country that experienced high infant and premature adult mortality, but the frequency with which children encountered death at a tender stage is striking. Novelist L.A.G. Strong, who wrote of his ecstatic summer childhoods in Sandycove, Dublin, recalled that his favourite saying was 'joy cometh in the morning' and that he would go to bed at night with these words on his lips, knowing that

> certain places, certain houses, seem lucky for us — nothing unpleasant happens to us while we are in their shelter. We cannot be unhappy, we cannot even be unwell. We thrive in them like plants in favourite soil (Strong, 1931, pp. 158, 193).

The experiences of Paddy Doyle were quite the opposite; he developed an obsession with death and

> because of the fear of dying that had been instilled from my first days in the school, the prayer I said most fervently each night was: 'If I should die before I wake'.

Transferred as a child from one hospital to another, his frequent encounters with death in these institutions had the most profound and frightening effect on him till he became immune, and accepted the ritual as part of each day (Doyle, 1988, p. 52). For those who had lost parents, death played a large part in their everyday thoughts.

Death seems contradictory for children — it scares them and yet they are drawn to it, often because those who have died have been people who were essential to their nurturing and well-being. Thus Doyle 'held on to other people's memories of the dead and hugged them close to me' (Doyle, 1988, p. 68). The force of Noel Browne's autobiography is different because it is punctuated with a seething anger at the sheer lack of humanity shown towards families wiped out by TB and the lack of official response to a disease which should have been rendered non-fatal by the state. Writing about his brother Jody, Browne reflected:

> Jody was unwanted, crippled, unable to fend for himself or communicate his simplest needs, except to the family. He was unable to mix with his peers. It is impossible to imagine the awesome humiliation and desperation of his life. I have never understood its purpose (Browne, 1986, p. 24).

There is a touch of this anger in Peter Sheridan's book, in the most effective part of the text, when he reflects on the loss of his brother Frankie as a result of a brain tumour, and the effect it had on his parents. What could a family do but pray?

> I blamed God for being the fat, lazy bastard he was. We'd said a million rosaries and he still hadn't lifted a finger (Sheridan, 1999, p. 225).

Death is all pervasive in McCourt's Limerick and reflected on ironically and angrily. Some of the most poignant and powerful sentences in the book read:

> My brothers are dead and my sister is dead. I wonder if they died for Ireland or the faith. Dad says they were too young to die for anything (McCourt, 1996, p. 113).

Death rates were to remain high, not only because proper health care in Ireland was effectively reserved for the wealthy but also because contraception was not an option. Lily O'Connor put it simply:

> Death was a part of our everyday life and we took it all in our stride . . . just as often as there were deaths in the tenements there were births (O'Connor, 2000, p. 25).

IX

Unsurprisingly, religion also pervades the memoirs of childhood and the authors' accounts of their engagement with it provide key insights into how this aspect of everyday life was interpreted by children. Common themes emerge repeatedly. Prominent among them is the solace children encountered in religion. It may seem strange that many children should receive comfort from a religion, some of whose clerical representatives were responsible for inflicting great suffering, but this would be to read childhood backwards. As well as fear, children experienced great comfort in religion and its institutional practices. In a rare gem of an essay, published in a collection of Irish writing in 1993, John McGahern, no stranger to the wrath of an intolerant church, reflected on what religion meant to him growing up in Leitrim. As an adult the belief may have dissipated, but as a child, he never found church ceremonies tedious. They gave him pleasure. For him, the movement of focus from the home and the school to the church brought with it a lightness, a lifting of oppression and a joy. He wrote emphatically:

> I have nothing but gratitude for the spiritual remnants of that upbringing, the sense of our origins beyond the bounds of sense, an awareness of mystery and wonderment, grace and sacrament and the absolute equality of all men and women underneath the sun of heaven (McGahern, 1993, p. 18).

Gene Kerrigan also suggests that religious fervour did little damage: 'we totally accepted that our every thought was being monitored by the great bugging agency in the sky', and did not feel suffocated by such policing, because in reality 'we knew little or nothing about religion' (Kerrigan, 1998, pp. 102 ff). This is a crucial point. Religion in the context of these childhoods was not about understanding, but about belonging, participation, inclusiveness, and, in some cases, escape — experiences that were all the more pronounced for children who had virtually nothing else to hold on to.

George O'Brien, in *The Village of Longing*, an account of his boyhood in Waterford in the 1950s presided over by a mother devoted to her Catholic faith, remembers that he too came to love the unity that religion brought: 'Being an altar boy was the first experience I had of completeness . . . the notion that the show couldn't go on without me gave rise to a feeling of integration.' Meanwhile, thinking temporarily that he had a religious vocation left him feeling 'extremely thankful and strangely cleansed' (O'Brien, 1987, pp. 94–116). But for many — and again this is where it's not always clear to what extent adult perspective shapes the memories being related — 'belonging' was accompanied by resentment at what the church had taken away from them, or how the institutional church had profited from their deprivation, or the effect of the violence of, in Patrick Touher's phrase, 'those bastards who wore a collar under the cloak of a Christian Brother' (Touher, 1991, p. 66). But Touher, an inmate of Artane, also suggested that the Brothers — bad eggs aside — were victims too. He concedes:

> the brothers were doing their best, within limited circumstances, in hard times and with frightening numbers. They had no luxury, nothing to look forward to except more of the same (Touher, 1991, p. 173).

Others writing memoirs sought to make sense of the ridiculous logic of, for example, groups of contemplative nuns, their lives shut off from the world, their love confined to God, being put in charge of children deprived of normal family life. Bernadette Fahey recounts the nuns in Goldenbridge predicting the children would turn out just like their 'fallen' mothers. 'It was,' she wrote, 'as if the nuns had a personal investment in the cycle of failure' (Fahey, 1999, p. 146). In John McGahern's experience, there was also a strong snobbery in evidence — the importance to the priest of being the big educated fish in the parochial pond:

> In those days it took considerable wealth to put a boy
> through Maynooth and they looked and acted as if they
> came from a line of swaggering, confident men who
> dominated field and market and whose only culture was
> cunning, money and brute force. Though they could be
> violently sentimental and generous at times, in their hearts
> they despised their own people (McGahern, 1993, p. 20).

In the context of material deprivation, Paul Smith's *Country-woman* provides an explicit denunciation of a church perceived to have failed to look after the human needs of its flock. Those administering the church's affairs are presented in the context of acute class divisions — a middle-class indulging in the sanctification of the deprivation experienced by the poorer classes. He trenchantly castigated

> the way they teach people to accept poverty as a way of
> life. To accept and endure brutality in the name of God. By
> telling us not to question at all, but to submit. Submit like
> animals (Smith, 1962, p. 138).

Nor were these observations confined to Catholics; Robert Harbinson in Presbyterian Ulster suggested that his church 'saw so many offspring coming into a hopeless and joyless world and had become indifferent' (Harbinson, 1960, p. 22). Perhaps inevitably, Angela McCourt finally snapped at the constant reiteration of the phrase 'God is good':

> Mam says she's sure God is good for someone somewhere
> but he hasn't been seen lately in the lanes of Limerick
> (McCourt, 1996, p. 145).

There is evidence too that most of those who stuck loyally to religious routine were not crushed or smothered with guilt when they occasionally lapsed. Rules, after all, were made to be broken, and if forgiveness could be sought and procured, why not break the rules again? Thus, Dermot Healy, after receiving absolution in confession, skips out of the church: 'Then with a giddy heart I stood on the steps of the Cathedral ready to start all over from scratch again' (Healy, 1996, p. 103). The multitude of these reflections are important in revealing how an institution, usually interpreted as monolithic and unyielding with a vice-like grip on all, did not in reality invoke a common response, or indeed faith, on the part of its audience. Writing of the preaching Redemptorists, John McGahern has noted that they were appreciated like horror novels:

> 'He'd raise the hair on your head', I heard often remarked with deep satisfaction. Poorer performers were described as 'watery'.

In the same vein, it should not be assumed that all those who trooped every Sunday to observe the ritual had real belief: 'we go to see all the other hypocrites' was the honest comment of some small farmers in the Leitrim of John McGahern's youth (McGahern, 1993).

X

Looking at these memoirs collectively, it could be contended that the most valuable contribution they make to our understanding of the evolution of modern Irish society is the light they shed on a rigid but multi-layered sequence of social divisions, perhaps the most under-acknowledged theme of independent Ireland and a glaring absence from most narratives of modern Irish history. In these memoirs, what it felt like to be a victim of class discrimination is given frequent powerful airings. Bernadette Fahey, for example, notes the irony of the fact that soon after she and her siblings were placed in an orphanage, supposedly because of their mother's inability to look after them, her mother was offered and took a job rearing the children of a wealthy business family in Dublin (Fahey, 1999, p. 146). Gene Kerrigan acknowledges that, alongside his own happy childhood,

> there were other childhoods . . . in truth desperate children being not raised, but dragged up in shitty circumstances. Their lives were bordered by drink, violence and neglect.

As a child, Kerrigan was introduced to what people deemed re-
spectable and how this affected the behaviour of the afflicted: his
Aunt Eileen was stricken with TB, but when travelling for hospital
check-ups she stayed on the bus until the stop after the hospital
'so people would not see her getting off at the TB stop' (Kerrigan,
1998, p. 76).

Tuberculosis, of course, was overwhelmingly the disease of
the poor, and the fact that health care was a class issue in Ireland
leaps out from the pages under consideration. Even amongst the
have-nots, further divisions operated. It was immensely important, and satisfying, it seems, for the poor to be able to distinguish
themselves from the poorer. Playwright Sean O'Casey, as a working-class Protestant child, recounted the first of his many visits to
hospital to seek solace for his tortured eyes. A woman next to his
mother pointed out that a man in the waiting room had black and
red tickets:

> 'Why is that now', says the mother; 'because he's a pauper,
> and doesn't as we do, pay for his treatment'. Johnny felt a
> glow of pride. He wasn't a pauper and he held the card of
> admission out so that all could see it was printed in black
> (O'Casey, 1939, p. 126).

Yet another harrowing scene from *The Countrywoman* witnesses
Tommy Tucker's desperate attempt to find his mother's un-
marked pauper's grave following her death in the County Home,
another tragic institutional manifestation of Ireland's public
health system (Smith, 1962, p. 327).

Robert Harbinson described the rigid class divisions that operated in Ulster in the late 1920s and fumed against the factory
owners, most of whom had grown rich on the sweat of the population of his street and others like it: 'It seemed to me that they
determined, every fat jock of them, that not a single penny would
they let fall from their tight fists' (Harbinson, 1960, p. 42). George
O'Brien vividly recalled the differences in the status of the poor in
1950s Waterford, between those in Main Street and those in the
Church Lane cabins. 'It was', he wrote, 'impossible not to be

struck by the unbridgeable, inscrutable gulf which the mere turn of a corner could evidently create'. He noticed that only poor people had to fetch and carry water in order to wash and eat. Having discovered the game of handball, he realised it was not the handball alley which drew him,

> but crossing the line to consort with the impoverished, sharing for a couple of hours their looser, unstylised, more dangerous life. I envied them. I had the beige, hand-knit sweaters and the cotton socks. But they had strength and fury and staying power. Nobody told them they had to do homework or to sit quiet and read a book — sensibly, since where would stillness get them? So they had plenty of time to develop their prowess (O'Brien, 1987, p. 42).

But he soon learned, through witnessing the effects of poverty and emigration, that though their life may have been hectic, its joy was brittle.

The desire to cross such an obvious class line is another recurrent theme, particularly with those born into wealth. L.A.G. Strong in *The Garden* envied the boys in rags fishing off Dun Laoghaire pier and wanted to join them; Enid Starkie resented being a 'lady's child' because the status seemed to bring nothing but restrictions and obligations and no corresponding privileges and pleasures. Thus she envied the railwayman's family living in a cottage beneath the garden wall (Starkie, 1949, p. 21). Moira Vershoyle, growing up in comfortable surroundings in Clare before the First World War, remembered childhood as a long, aimless process of days with nothing to do. On a trip she jealously observed the slum children

> sitting on the kerb on the outskirts of Limerick. They sat with their bare feet in the gutter, pinching and pushing, laughing and screaming, runny-eyed and filthy-haired, but living a great life it seemed to me (Vershoyle, 1960, pp. 135–6).

Vershoyle's perception as a child that they were having a great life is understandable. She defined herself by opposition: she, seemingly incarcerated, they allowed do what they liked. But of course those children were the ones ultimately trapped, locked into a rigid class system from which few escaped. Kerrigan noted that

> there were things that were not talked about back then, though they were no secret. For instance, there was a right way to be born and a wrong way. And those who came here the wrong way, and their mothers, were risking stone-faced rejection and years of misery (Kerrigan, 1998, p. 205).

Bernadette Fahey, one of the many who came the 'wrong way', was one of the victims who ultimately found her treatment so suffocating that she left the country. The most powerful passage in her book articulates the reasons why:

> I left Ireland for several reasons, chief amongst which was the feeling that I didn't belong to anyone, anything or anywhere. I was also sick and tired of being asked where I came from and who I was. In common with hundreds of others who were raised in orphanages, I was ashamed of my past and did all in my power to hide it. England was a useful place to evade these issues. It was less parochial. People were happy enough to know which country you came from and leave it at that. For that reason alone it became the safe haven of thousands of orphans who couldn't bear the daily pressures that Irish society put on them. We were constantly confronted with our lack of roots and identity. This was extremely painful in a society that laid so much emphasis on one's family pedigree, place of birth and religious persuasion. These were the barometers by which individuals, families and groups were acceptable or not (Fahey, 1999, p. 194).

Class discrimination also emerges as a notable feature of the education system. Those from a deprived background clearly experienced more violence in the classroom than others. Colm Luibhéid, educated by the Jesuits at Belvedere, noted the occasional use of a leather strap, but remembered there was nothing humiliating about this form of punishment, because they were aware that more serious violence was the hallmark of other city schools. More significantly, he wrote,

> we noticed too that stupidity was never a crime and that, however much exasperation it might provoke in this or that teacher, the student in question was never made to believe that he was somehow an inferior being (Luibhéid, 1970, p. 123).

For Seán Dunne in working-class Waterford, 'the aim was to avoid a blow rather than know a lot' (Dunne, 1991, p. 43). Annabel Goff, an upper class lover of literature growing up with her Anglo-Irish family in Cork in the 1950s, resented being taught by women she felt were unqualified to impart learning because they were from the wrong social class. It was, she suggested 'poverty, failure to marry and hormonal imbalances which had brought these unfortunate women into the field of education' (Goff, 1990, p. 185 ff). Writing of his school life in Ballinrobe, Noel Browne noted with disgust how natives of the Gaeltacht were deemed socially inferior and that

> in spite of the fact that here was the true repository of the cherished native language, they were not favoured by our militant nationalist Christian Brothers, but treated with contempt as members of a lower order (Browne, 1986, p. 31).

As well as revealing different treatment according to class background, approaches to education suggest it was usually seen not in terms of its capacity to develop or enhance children's perception and experience, or indeed, imagination, but to emphasise limits. For those in day schools it seemed education was about regurgitation without thought. Ciaran Carson noted that 'we were constantly interrogated, since much of our routine learning was by rote. Rote did not end with primary school' (Carson, 1998, p. 212). John McGahern, later himself a teacher, took a subtle swipe at a jaded philosophy of education in *The Barracks*, when the father, Reegan, asked what they had learnt in school that day:

> Neither could they think of anything; they had experienced
> nothing; all they had heard was fact after fact; that nine
> nines were 81; that the London they didn't know was built
> on the Thames they didn't know (McGahern, 1993, p. 46).

Difficult or challenging issues were avoided. Gene Kerrigan, for
example, did not discover there had been a civil war in Ireland
until the age of 19, ensuring he would never believe the official
version of anything again (Kerrigan, 1998, pp. 166–7).

XII

This discouraging of questioning goes to the heart of the experience of many of these childhoods and indeed, it could be argued,
is a reason why many of the memoirs were written. It is almost as
if the process gave authors a forum to raise the questions they
were not encouraged or allowed to ask as children. Many of those
who wrote memoirs came through extreme experiences, yet they
managed to educate themselves and to question the limits and
parameters that were imposed in the environments in which they
were reared. Many criticise the prevailing climate in which they
were denied the opportunity to articulate.

It has to be reiterated that there are different reasons why
these memoirs were written. If such reasons were to be labelled, it
could be asserted that they fall into four categories: those who
wrote of a burdened childhood, and tell of survival amidst harshness or to confront the silences of the past (for example, Flynn,
McCourt, Doyle and Fahey); those who wrote of childhood to
perpetuate a fantasy (O'Connor and Taylor); those who recorded
sometimes fraught but essentially ordinary childhoods, and who
can look back with equanimity and without an agenda (Kerrigan,
O'Connor, O'Brien, Sheridan); and those distinguished writers
who wrote their memoirs in the context of wider reflections on the
society around them — in other words, those who carve out a distinctive literary voice and reflect maturely and with distance
(McGahern, Healy, Smith). Collectively, the writers give insight to
the dilemmas facing all classes of children.

Kerrigan notes that 'smug, self-satisfied Ireland did not want confident children, assertive or adventurous children, and fading into the background where you were seen and not heard was a cardinal virtue' (Kerrigan, 1998, p. 27). Barely seen and never heard is also an apt summation of the experiences of those in industrial schools. Seán Maher's childhood as a traveller was marked by a challenging of the idea that in the end the child can only continue as his parents did before him. He was seen as odd, and upset the routine of travelling life, because, as he remembers, 'he wanted answers and reasons for everything' (Maher, 1972, p. 72). Those growing up in a liberal environment were given answers and reasons, but most did not have that luxury because anything difficult was at best ignored, at worst, stigmatised. 'The emotions we felt as schoolgirls', wrote Nuala O'Faoláin, 'were volatile and exaggerated, and they have always been despised by the world. But they were not trivial' (O'Faoláin, 1996, p. 40).

Some, like George O'Brien, whatever about material circumstances, were luckier, not only because of their advanced reading at an early age, but because

> I firmly believed that whatever crossed my mind had to be aired immediately, if not sooner. Moreover, I belonged to a household where there was continual clamour for free speech (O'Brien, 1987, p. 23).

In contrast, Frank McCourt was to find again and again that 'big people don't like questions from children' (McCourt, 1996, p. 102). Therein lies the value of these memoirs, and indeed their validity as an essential source. Not only do they deconstruct many of the myths which Irish society sponsored and promoted. They also raise many of the questions that will have to be tackled by those intent on writing meaningful and critical histories of modern Ireland. This is not to say that they are completely representative of the experience of Irish childhood. But it is to say that they give us a whole raft of source material which, like other source material, must be used carefully. In this context, memoirs raise the question of the extent to which we trust our evidence or source material. Is there any reason why we should completely trust memos and documents prepared by generations of civil servants? Are they too not products of their time, capable of displaying bias and subjectivity?

The challenge, philosophical as much as historical, is to fit the memoirs into a framework of research which recognises the validity of a cross-referential approach. The begrudgers who insist Frank McCourt exaggerated the poverty of Limerick would find ample evidence of the stark poverty he described if they consulted Limerick Corporation's Medical Officer's reports from the era. And therein lies the value of the memoirs of childhood in twentieth-century Ireland: not only do we have the official record of what happened, we also have a record of what it felt like. We can, as a result, aspire to a history that is more complete and ultimately more human.

References

Browne, Noel C. (1986). *Against the Tide*. Dublin: Gill and Macmillan.

Burke, Eimear (1990). 'The treatment of working class children in Dublin by statutory and voluntary organisations 1889–1922'. Unpublished MA thesis, University College Dublin.

Carson, Ciaran (1998). *The Star Factory*. London: Granta.

Cowan, Peadar (1960). *Dungeons Deep*. Dublin: Peadar Cowan.

Coyle, Kathleen (1943). *The Magical Realm: An Irish Childhood*. New York: E.P. Dutton.

Dáil Debates, 23 April 1954.

Devlin, Edith Newman (2000). *Speaking Volumes: A Dublin Childhood*. Belfast: Blackstaff.

Doyle, Paddy (1988). *The God Squad*. Dublin: Raven Arts Press.

Dunne, Seán (1991). *In My Father's House*. Oldcastle, Co. Meath: Gallery Books.

Fahey, Bernadette (1999). *Freedom of Angels: Surviving Goldenbridge Orphanage*. Dublin: O'Brien Press.

Flynn, Mannix (1983). *Nothing to Say*. Dublin: Ward River Press.

Goff, Annabel (1990). *Walled Gardens: Scenes from an Anglo-Irish Childhood*. London: Macmillan.

Harbinson, Robert (1960, 3rd ed. 1987). *No Surrender: An Ulster Childhood*. Belfast: Blackstaff.

Healy, Dermot (1996). *The Bend for Home*. London: Harvill Press.

Kennedy, Finola (2000). 'The suppression of the Carrigan Report: A historical perspective on child abuse' in *Studies* 89, No. 356, pp. 354–63.

Kerrigan, Gene (1998). *Another Country: Growing up in 1950s Ireland*. Dublin: Gill and Macmillan.

Kiberd, Declan (1995). *Inventing Ireland: The Literature of the Modern Nation*. London: Cape.

Luibhéid, Colm (1990). *Magical Realm*. Loxlow: Pall Mall Press.

Maher, Seán (1972). *The Road to God Knows Where: A Memoir of a Travelling Boyhood*. Dublin: Talbot Press.

McCourt, Frank (1996). *Angela's Ashes: Memoir of a Childhood*. London: Harper Collins.

McGahern, John (1963). *The Barracks*. London: Faber.

McGahern, John (1993). 'The church and its spire' in Colm Tóibín (ed.) *Soho Square 6*. London: Bloomsbury.

McGearty, Claire (1995). 'A study of the history of charity children in Ireland 1868–1980'. Unpublished MA thesis, University College Dublin.

McGill, Patrick (1914). *Children of the Dead: The Autobiography of an Irish Navvy*. London: H. Jenkins.

McKay, Susan (1998). *Sophia's Story*. Dublin: Gill and Macmillan.

National Archives of Ireland, DE 2/84, 3 May 1921.

National Society for the Protection Cruelty to Children, *Annual Report* 1944-45, pp. 1963–68.

O'Brien, George (1987). *The Village of Longing*. Mullingar: Lilliput Press.

O'Casey, Sean (1939). *I Knock at the Door*. London: Macmillan.

O'Connor, Lily (2000). *Can Lily O'Shea Come out to Play?* Dingle: Brandon.

O'Connor, Rory (2000). *Gander at the Gate*. Dublin: Lilliput Press.

O'Faoláin, Nuala (1996). *Are You Somebody*? Dublin: New Island.

O'Sullivan, Eoin and Raftery, Mary (1999). *Suffer the Little Children: The Inside Story of Ireland's Industrial Schools*. Dublin: New Island.

O'Sullivan, Maurice (1953). *Twenty Years a Growing*. Oxford: Oxford University Press.

Richardson, Joanna (1973). *Enid Starkie*. London: John Murray.

Sheridan, Peter (1999). *44: A Dublin Memoir*. London: Macmillan.

Smith, Paul (1962). *The Countrywoman*. London: Picador.

Starkie, Enid (1949). *A Lady's Child*. London: Faber and Faber.

Strong, L.A.G. (1931). *The Garden*. London: Victor Gollanz.

Sunday Tribune, 18 June 2000.

Taylor, Alice (1988). *To School through the Fields: An Irish Country Childhood*. Dingle: Brandon.

Touher, Patrick (1991). *Fear of the Collar: Artane Industrial School*. Dublin: O'Brien Press.

Vershoyle, Moira (1960). *So Long to Wait: An Irish Childhood*. London: G. Bles.

Wyley, Roisín (1992). 'Changing attitudes to children: The state's role in the status and welfare of children, 1952–87'. Unpublished MA thesis, University College Dublin.

Chapter 5

Too Much Knowledge, Too Much Fear: Curricular Developments in Irish Primary Schools[1]

Mark Morgan

The theme of this paper is that the experiences of children in school are driven by societal influences that have resulted in too many subject areas and too many sub-topics within these areas of learning. Within this broad theme I will argue that fears for our children have resulted in a curriculum that, paradoxically, prepares them less well in a social and personal sense than might otherwise be the case. The perspective of my critique is modern social and cognitive psychology (Bandura, 1997). This branch of psychology is concerned with how information is acquired and applied and the particular influences that are important in behavioural change, with a special focus on changes that result from curricular experiences.

The Context

Since my critique will suggest the need for substantial changes in the kind of experiences that children have in school, it would be

---

[1] Thanks are due to Joe Dunne and Ann Looney for discussions on an earlier draft.

ahistorical if I did not acknowledge the major improvements in the education system that have taken place over the last three decades. In fact, I would suggest that part of the problem may be that the success of the system in producing our recently found prosperity has prompted demands on the system which it may be beyond its capacity to deliver.

John Macnamara in 1967 produced what was probably the first published piece of controversial educational research in Ireland when he showed that Irish children at age 14 had roughly the same level of English as an English child at age 11 years (Macnamara, 1967). While we might disagree with Macnamara's interpretation — to the effect that this had to do with bilingualism and the fact that Irish children had to carry two languages — it is beyond dispute that there was evidence of serious problems with the level of English at the time. In contrast, recent international comparisons now place Ireland at a level that our social and economic development justifies, and indicate that Irish children tend to do rather better in language (English) than do comparable English samples (Martin and Morgan, 1994).

Later I will criticise the Revised Curriculum on the grounds that there are too many subjects. Yet when we had only three core subjects, as defined by the Primary Certificate examination abolished in 1967, not everyone achieved a satisfactory standard in those subjects. In fact, about 20 per cent of children never reached sixth class because of the requirement that children in sixth had to sit the examination (Primary Curriculum Review Body, 1990). The 'early school leaving' of the 1960s meant something much more basic than is the case in more recent times when it refers to failure to complete post-primary education.

Another positive aspect appertains to the ability of students admitted into teaching in the Colleges of Education. While the proportion of men has fallen, it is striking that in relative terms the cohort of students being admitted is at the same high level of ability in terms of Leaving Certificate performance that was traditionally associated with teacher training. The fact that teachers see themselves as a high-ability group has been shown to be especially important in terms of teachers' sense of what they can achieve within the system and specifically to their sense of collective efficacy, that is, the teachers' views on what they can bring about within the system (Goddard, Hoy and Hoy, 2000).

The third positive feature has to do with children's attitude to school. The debate about the success or failure of the 1971 'New' Curriculum has resulted in a total consensus on one point, viz. that children enjoy going to school much more than they did before the curricular change of that era (Primary Curriculum Review Body, 1990). The importance of this attitudinal change should not be underestimated.

My views on the current experiences of children in primary school, and of their experience of the curriculum in particular, hinge on two central and related matters. The first is that children are expected to learn too many subjects within which there are too many topics. The second is that out of fear for children, we have loaded the curriculum with subject matter that schools cannot deal with and which, in some cases, limits children's capacity to deal with the very concerns that have given rise to the fears in the first place.

TOO MANY SUBJECTS

The 1971 New Curriculum almost doubled the number of subjects on the primary school curriculum and this has been followed in turn by a further increase in the Revised Curriculum (Department of Education and Science, 1999). Moreover, there is little to suggest that this tendency to increase the number of subjects is diminishing on the evidence of current interest in three areas. One is information technology, which is becoming more relevant as schools become better equipped. Modern languages are also proposed, although on a pilot basis initially. The third is Social, Personal and Health Education, which incorporates (among other features) the Stay Safe programme, the Relationships and Sexuality Programme and the Substance Misuse Prevention Programme ('Walk Tall').

These changes have been accompanied by a recognition of the need to accommodate diversity, and not merely individual differences but also differences that are based on the belief that the learning responses of some children are qualitatively different from those of others, as in the case of 'dyslexia' and 'attention deficit disorder'. This expansion of the ways relevant differences are conceptualised is a related but different topic that is worthy of consideration on another occasion.

Paralleling the expansion in the curriculum, a number of developments have brought about a decline in the instructional time available to teachers in the primary system. The first factor in this is the age of leaving primary school. For a variety of reasons, including the abolition of the practice of holding children back, nearly all children finish primary school while they are still 12 years old. This contrasts with 30 years ago when the age was closer to 13.5 or even 14 years.

Another influence of the same nature has come about as a result of the redefinition of the school year from the requirement to take 50 vacation days to a requirement to have 180 school days. It was an unnoticed effect that this brought about a decline in the length of the school year. Traditionally it was not unusual for school to manage over 190 days.

The third and largely unmonitored factor is the low school attendance that is a feature of some areas, which effectively reduces teacher-student contact. This is so significant that it has been used as an indicator of disadvantage in a Department of Education and Science initiative ('Breaking the Cycle'). It is also worth noting difficulties of enforcing the law as well as the fact that the law regarding school attendance does not apply to children under six years so that absences in infant classes are deemed irrelevant.

CONSEQUENCES

This expansion of the curriculum has several consequences for teachers, for students and for the system. Perhaps the most serious is that there is evidence to suggest that in trying to get some coverage of every topic, attention afforded to higher order skills such as comprehension, comparison, and inference has diminished. In a comparative study of the teaching of literacy skills, it is of particular interest that Irish teachers accord relatively less attention to higher order skills than their counterparts in many European countries (Martin and Morgan, 1994).

A second consequence of the overcrowding of the curriculum is that the knowledge acquired tends to remain inert and is not applied in contexts where it might be relevant. An example of this phenomenon is worth mentioning. This has to do with mathematics in applied settings. There is considerable evidence that the strategies used in everyday life bear little resemblance to what people learn in school. Rather, what is learned in school remains confined to that (school) context. In applied settings people learn new strategies that are specific to situations, and that bear little resemblance to the formal procedures learned in school (Myers, 1993).

A third consequence is that the overcrowding of the curriculum may contribute to children leaving primary school without key basic skills. By 'basic' is meant not the rote learning of skills in spelling and learning 'tables', but rather those skills that are essential for further learning. The initial evidence of this came from a study of primary school-leavers in the 1970s when teachers were posed a series of questions regarding the ability of individual students to cope with the literacy demands of society/post-primary school. It emerged that (depending on the particular skill involved) some 5–8 per cent were judged by their teachers to be unable to cope with the literacy demands of everyday life or post-primary school (Fontes and Kellaghan, 1977). What is especially important, however, is that despite the improvement in average standards (referred to above) the percentage of pupils judged by their teachers to have these basic literacy problems has remained stubbornly around the level identified in the 1970s (Cosgrove, Kellaghan, Forde and Morgan, 2000).

While the extent to which the overcrowding of the curriculum contributes to this problem is not easy to establish, recent curricular developments are an important part of the context within which this problem has to be addressed. One of the problems that confounds the overcrowding at primary level is the number of subjects at post-primary which, according to recent evidence, can be between 13 and 18 subjects in first year (NCCA, 1999). With this number of subjects there is no mechanism for deciding what is central in all of the material to be learned.

Another major issue is non-implementation. There is considerable evidence (especially in the drug prevention area) that the failure of programmes is often directly related to the failure to put them into effect. When schools are divided into those that delivered and did not deliver a programme, effects are found in the situation where the programme is faithfully implemented (Paglia and Room, 1999).

There is little evidence on how teachers are coping with the increase in the curriculum. There are indications that schools or individual teachers make their own decisions as to what is core and what is peripheral (Primary Curriculum Review Body, 1990). The recently published evaluation of the Relationships and Sexuality Programme (Morgan, 2000) showed that while there was agreement among parents and teachers on the need for an RSE programme, and a broad consensus on the principles on which the programmes should be based (age-appropriate information, linking RSE with values etc.), and even on the topics that should be included in a programme (understanding birth and new life), a great many schools are not implementing the programme in classrooms. What is especially interesting is that when teachers were asked about the obstacles to actual implementation in schools, the 'overcrowded curriculum' was cited as the major reason. Interestingly, while less than one-quarter of primary teachers took the view that 'vigorous objections' against RSE were a major factor, nearly three-quarters cited the overcrowded curriculum as a major obstacle.

The other consequence is in terms of teacher preparation, which has seen the demands on students studying for the Bachelor of Education degree at least double since the first graduates in

1977. What has happened is that the programme has grown in response to curricular developments in primary schools, so that the expansion of the B.Ed. has paralleled the increases in the number of subjects in the curriculum.

It is perhaps significant that this expansion shows no signs of abating, at least in terms of the demands on schools and the demands on the colleges to prepare students specifically for new areas of learning or emerging societal problems. In response to recent Dáil questions, St Patrick's College was asked to provide information on how B.Ed. students were being prepared to deal with drug problems, bullying and equipping teachers to deal with children who were bereaved. What is especially significant is that the information sought was not of a general kind; the requests were for the specific information and skills students were being equipped with in relation to the particular matter of concern.

FEAR

It is worth looking at the historical context of the fears that people have always had for their children. Parents, in particular, have always had fears *for* their children and fears *of* their children. This is usually manifested in concerns about features of contemporary life and especially of popular culture that are perceived as dangerous. Over 100 years ago the first comics ('Penny Dreadfuls') were thought likely to corrupt the youth of Victorian England. Jazz was seen as highly dangerous in the 1930s and Elvis Presley's hip movements were deemed a major hazard in 1956, as evidenced by the conditions set down by the TV company which broadcast his first major appearance, viz., that he should be shown only from the waist upwards. It is fair to say that the concerns over the portrayal of violence on television are at least partly influenced by these fears since the broad thrust of the evidence is that while filmed violence may have some minor impact on aggressiveness it is much less significant than other influences in the family and community (Bandura, 1997).

The problem comes about when the concerns of society translate into a call for a new subject or the expansion of a school subject in the curriculum. In 2001, for instance, there were widely publicised calls for suicide prevention programmes, cancer prevention, programmes to improve diet, crime prevention, media awareness, and for courses dealing with depression as well as driver awareness and skills. These are in addition to the topics of the Stay Safe programme, as well as the prevention of drug and alcohol misuse, and programmes like Exploring Masculinities in post-primary schools.

My first difficulty with these is that it is simply not possible to continue to add to a curriculum that is already more than full. Potentially, the number of courses can go on indefinitely, if only because our awareness of societal problems changes independently of whether or not a particular problem is becoming more or less urgent (Myers, 1993).

My second and more basic objection is that these additional 'subjects' are ineffective, at best. The evidence in relation to drug education is especially interesting in this regard. There is a considerable body of evidence to show that attempts to prevent drug use by pointing out the associated dangerous consequences does not work and, in some circumstances, actually increases the likelihood of experimentation (Paglia and Room, 1999). Personally, I was struck by the real limits of such tactics through my involvement in a project with young heroin users from the North Inner-City. Half of these young people had lost a parent as a result of heroin, and all could name at least two people who died directly as a result of heroin. Yet all of them said that when they started, their view was that 'I can handle this'.

There is also evidence that such an approach can be counterproductive as has been shown with some suicide prevention programmes. With 900 deaths from suicide in the last two years and suicide being the leading cause of death among males in the age group 16 to 25 years, it is understandable that people should look to the school to deal with such a frightening problem. However, this should not imply that we have a programme that will successfully rise to the challenge. The evidence from evaluations of such programmes is that they tend in some cases to result in higher levels of suicidal ideation, i.e. thinking about suicide (Garland and Zigler, 1993), which is one of the single strongest predictors of actual suicide. What seems to happen is that the attempts to destigmatise suicide portray it as a reaction to the stresses of adolescence (problems with parents and teachers), and thus carry a message that is exactly the opposite of what is intended. Similarly, curriculum-based programmes have in some cases been known to exaggerate the frequency of suicide so that it becomes a more common and therefore acceptable act (Garland and Zigler, 1993). Thus, there is a sense in which such programmes can have an 'agenda setting' effect, and while this may be desirable for some problems or only mildly problematic for others, in the case of suicide the effect is exactly the opposite of what is intended. In other words, counterproductive effects are likely from programmes that focus on discussing problems rather than dealing with the underlying difficulties that cause them. A productive approach is to tackle the causes of the problem in question rather than merely to talk about it or to give information regarding it.

Fortunately, school can make worthwhile inroads into many of the problems that it is asked to deal with. An interesting angle comes from those interventions that have been most effective in dealing with societal problems like criminality and drug use. It is now evident that one of the best approaches is to prevent school failure. This is the interesting outcome of evaluations of programmes that were targeted at preventing young children from disadvantaged backgrounds from falling behind in school (Zigler et al., 1992). Some of the 'Head Start' programmes have also been shown to have long-term positive effects in preventing substance abuse and criminality, even though their main target was the prevention of school failure in the early years. It would seem that one of the most effective ways to prevent anti-social behaviour is not to teach about anti-social behaviour but rather to teach basic skills in school.

This conclusion is supported by ongoing study of literacy in prisons. The pilot results indicate that the majority of prisoners have very poor literacy skills and are close to what was traditionally called 'illiterate'. I am not suggesting that school failure and subsequent illiteracy is the only cause or even the main cause of the series of events that leads to prison. Rather, what seems to be the case is that school failure reduces choices in a way that increases the probability that individuals will embark on such a pathway.

A very similar point emerged in the International Adult Literacy Survey (IALS) that examined the connection between social life and literacy skills (Morgan, Hickey and Kellaghan, 1997). People who had good literacy skills were more likely to be involved in a range of activities that apparently had little to do with literacy, like involvement in sport and community activities and even social activities like going to films or plays. Remarkably, people with good literacy activities were more likely to participate in sporting activities. On the other hand, people with poor skills tended only to watch television for longer periods. The important point is that basic skills like literacy have pervasive effects on social life and exert perhaps more of an effect on social activities than any new programme that we might dream up. The implication of what I am saying is that we do not need informational school programmes about crime or dire warnings about what a life of crime brings. Rather, school can make a major contribution by maximising students' success and preventing failure. Put simply, I disagree with the idea that where there is a problem there is a niche/subject corresponding to that problem.

SOCIETAL FEARS, CAUTION AND RISK-TAKING

There may also be an unintended outcome of our societal fears, which can have unfortunate consequences for the personal development of children. This can come about if there is such an overriding concern about safety that it limits the possibility of children experiencing feelings like failure, sadness, and disappointment. It is an intrinsic part of personal development that children feel sad, anxious and angry. An excessive concern about safety and avoiding failure can result in children being afraid to be wrong, afraid to fail, and thus being unable to deal with such problems when they are encountered.

In this regard I wish to make three suggestions to help develop the type of experiences that children might have in order to promote personal development. Firstly, the experience of failure is inevitable and learning to cope with failure, rather than trying to avoid it, is crucial. A second, and related point is that the highest levels of motivation are to be found in those tasks that challenge us most, where we sometimes encounter difficulties, setbacks and even failures, when these are 'mixed' with success (Bandura, 1997). We know that the growth of feelings of self-efficacy is a major contributor to learning, to seeking challenges and to achievement. And thirdly, the enhancement of self-esteem does not contribute greatly to personal development. It is not my intention to devalue the self-esteem movement but rather to suggest that it may be starting from the wrong point. It emphasises how a child feels rather than what they do and ignores the importance of mastery/persistence in overcoming frustration. It is true that low self-esteem is often associated with failure, with dropping out from school and with addiction problems. However, the results of a considerable body of research show that low self-esteem is the consequence rather than the cause of the lack of competence in these areas.

Before we leave the topic of how societal fears influence schools and the curriculum, it is salutary to observe that other ways of making people aware of problems in society (other than through schools) have not always proven effective. Very often the mass media are involved and sometimes the outcomes are quite inappropriate. Specifically, what tends to happen is that the target of the fear is unidentified or that a counter-productive general caution is generated. An example is to be found in the case of child sexual abuse. While the evidence consistently indicates that most cases of abuse (over 95 per cent) are within the family, the greatest fear generated is of paedophiles who are also strangers.

The other consequence also associated with the concern about child sexual abuse is an undue level of caution among people dealing with children. It may be necessary for teachers to ensure that their dealings with children are above suspicion, but if these extend to fear of picking up a child who has fallen or comforting a child in distress, then childhood will have lost significantly.

IMPLICATIONS AND NEW DIRECTIONS

What are the practical implications of the problems identified here? Obviously, acceptance of the argument put forward would have major implications for curricular change and development at a national level, as well as for the relationships between the various educational sectors, viz. primary, post-primary and third level. Yet, some of the implications of my arguments can briefly be sketched.

For a beginning, there is a need to identify the basic skills, knowledge and competencies in the various subject areas. This is a major task that should not be confused with traditional views about 'basics'. In this context, 'basic' refers to those elements of learning that are the building blocks for subsequent learning. The key question will then become: what are the basic forms of learning that children need in order to master the areas of learning that they will encounter later in primary school and in post-primary and higher education?

The extent of this problem has become clear to me from my involvement in the study of non-completion in courses in higher education carried out at the Educational Research Centre (Morgan, Flanagan and Kellaghan, 2001). One of the interesting findings was that courses with a mathematical content (computer studies, science, and engineering) have a substantially higher rate of non-completion than courses without such a content (business studies, law and humanities). A follow-up study is indicating a major problem of non-continuity in students' learning of mathematics at primary and post-primary levels. Specifically, the basic concepts learned at primary level are not built on at post-primary, resulting in the need for third-level courses to include 'basic content'.

A second important way in which 'basic' skills and competencies are exemplified is demonstrated by some features of the Social, Personal and Health Education programme (SPHE) that has recently been introduced in primary and post-primary schools. In this curriculum, the central personal and social skills that are important in a variety of situations, including decision-making, assertiveness and expression of feelings, have been identified. Furthermore, the context in which these are applied is varied and age-appropriate. Finally, there are a variety of techniques to try to ensure that the skills have a real-life dimension and do not remain as inert knowledge. The danger with this programme from the perspective of the present paper is that it will become so diversified through the effort to deal with new problems that the core of basic skills will be lost.

The third positive development is the re-conceptualisation of old-fashioned concepts of which the re-invention of 'literacy' is a good example. Traditionally, people were categorised as being 'literate' or 'illiterate' on the basis of a crude indicator such as being able to read to a certain level. Modern conceptions of literacy have forsaken this absolute conception and regard literacy as a broad set of competencies encompassing several functions. This has a number of implications. Firstly, there are domains of literacy that correspond to areas in which literacy skills are relevant, including prose literacy, document literacy, quantitative literacy and scientific literacy. Secondly, there is a recognition that literacy frequently involves higher order skills, including comprehension, inference and comparison, rather than simply the decoding of print. The idea of identifying skills across the curriculum is certainly one that is worth pursuing.

CONCLUSION

I have argued that the expansion of the curriculum has reached a point where any further increases would be counter-productive.

Within this broad theme I have looked in particular at some kinds of societal problems that schools are supposed to address. I have taken the view that while schools often have something to contribute to the solution of these problems, it may be inappropriate to think that for every problem there is a slice of curriculum that can address that particular problem.

References

Bandura, A. (1997). *Self-efficacy: The Exercise of Control*. New York: W.H. Freeman.

Cosgrove, J., Kellaghan, T., Forde, P., and Morgan, M. (2000). *The 1998 National Assessment of English Reading*. Dublin: Educational Research Centre.

Department of Education and Science (1999). *Primary School Curriculum*. Dublin: Government Publications.

Fontes, P.J. and Kellaghan, T. (1977). 'Incidence and correlates of illiteracy in Irish primary schools'. *Irish Journal of Education*, 11, pp. 5–20.

Garland, A.F. and Zigler, E. (1993). 'Adolescent suicide prevention: Current research and social policy implications'. *American Psychologist*, Vol. 48, pp. 169–182.

Goddard, R.D., Hoy, W.K. and Hoy, A.W. (2000). 'Collective teacher efficacy: Its meaning, measure, and impact on student achievement'. *American Educational Research Journal*, Vol. 37, pp. 479–507.

Macnamara, J. (1967). *Bilingualism and Primary Education*. London: Edinburgh University Press.

Martin, M. and Morgan, M. (1994). 'Reading literacy in Ireland: A comparative analysis of the IEA reading literacy study'. *Irish Journal of Education*, Vol. 28, pp. 3–101.

Morgan, M., Hickey, B. and Kellaghan, T. (1997). *International Adult Literacy Survey: Results for Ireland (A Report to the Minister for Education)*. Dublin: Government Stationery Office.

Morgan, M. (2000). *Relationships and Sexuality Education Programme: An Evaluation and Review of Implementation*. Dublin: Department of Education and Science.

Morgan, M., Flanagan, R. and Kellaghan, T. (2001). *A Study of Non-completion in Undergraduate University Courses.* Dublin: Higher Education Authority.

Myers, D.M. (1993). *Social Psychology.* New York: McGraw-Hill.

National Council for Curriculum and Assessment (1999). *Junior Cycle Review.* Dublin: NCCA.

Paglia, A. and Room, R. (1999). 'Preventing substance use problems among youth: A literature review and recommendations'. *The Journal of Primary Prevention,* 20, pp. 3–50.

Primary Curriculum Review Body (1990). *Report.* Dublin: NCCA.

Zigler, E., Taussig, C. and Black, K. (1992). 'Early Childhood Intervention: A promising preventative for juvenile delinquency'. *American Psychologist,* 47, pp. 997–1006.

Chapter 6

CHAOTIC GIRLHOOD: NARRATIVES OF JEWISH GIRL SURVIVORS OF TRANSNISTRIA[1]

Ronit Lentin

INTRODUCTION: 'I REMAINED'

Everyone had typhus . . . from one hundred and twenty people, eighteen remained. *I remained* . . . My little brother who had a chest infection choked. My big brother took my little brother, put him into a sack, put it on his back and brought him to the grave. A sort of hole where they threw . . . the dead. . . . My eldest brother managed to mount the cart with my aunt and uncle. . . . And he wanted us to come too. We never saw him again . . . (Bertha Abrahami).[2]

[1] My thanks are extended firstly to the women who agreed to share their experiences with me and to Yitzhak Yalon and Yitzhak Arzi who put me in touch with survivors. Secondly, I would like to thank the Arts and Humanities Benefaction Fund, Trinity College Dublin, for financial assistance that enabled me to do fieldwork for this project. Thanks also to Denise Roman for her erudite comments on an earlier draft and to Professor Dalia Ofer, Director of the Vidal Sassoon International Centre for the Study of Antisemitism, Hebrew University Jerusalem, and to Dr Michael Shafir, Radio Free Europe/Radio Liberty, Prague, for their assistance.

[2] Quotes from Bertha Abrahami and Martha Ellenbogen are taken from interviews I conducted with them in Israel in Spring 2000. The translations from Hebrew are mine.

Speaking the sounds of a long silence, the silence that was the Shoah, has been my obsession for many years. When did I begin wanting to put sounds to the chaos that was the silence about the Shoah? When did my journey beyond my apparently 'normal' Israeli childhood begin?

Some childhoods are dominated by silence; yet the child — enveloped in that silence — is often barely aware of the silence because of the din of the voices around her. Because this was my childhood, I have made it my life's work to excavate that silence. But the deeper I dig, the dimmer the sounds of silence become. Memories of murder and devastation, robbed childhoods, 'survivor guilt', amazement at the horrors and marvel that they had survived, all speak in the words of women who survived Transnistria, whom I quote throughout this paper.

I was born in Palestine under the British Mandate at the end of 'that' war, and grew up in Israel. My family comes from Bukovina, today divided between northern Romania and southern Ukraine. My own parents left Romania 'in time' — Father came to Palestine in the 1920s and Mother left Czernowitz (today Chernivtsy in Ukraine) in the last week it was possible for Jews to leave freely. With her parents and brother, Mother spent a year as a refugee before they made it to Palestine in 1941. My parents were married in Tel Aviv in 1943 and did all they could to give their three children a 'normal' Israeli childhood. They did not speak about the Shoah, and only when their relatives began arriving in Israel in the 1950s did I first hear the Transnistria word. I heard it, but I was not ready to listen.

Unbeknownst to me, however, Transnistria had been imprinted on my memory. As the Israeli writer and daughter of survivors, Nava Semel, says:

> [F]or years, since I was a child, I heard the name Transnistria, Transnistria. I wasn't sure it was a real place. But Transnistria *does* exist (Simyonovics, 1999).

Transnistria was imprinted on my childish mind as I heard, but did not listen to, the conversations of Mother's relatives who sur-

vived it. Studying family photographs of people whose relatives
were murdered during the Shoah, Marianne Hirsch (1997) coined
the concept of 'postmemory'. Family photographs, she argued, are
documents of both memory (the survivor's) and 'postmemory' (of
the child of survivors). Photographs, such as those included in Art
Spiegelman's Holocaust cartoon *Maus*, become sites of remembrance, 'mixed, hybrid . . . bound intimately with life and death,
with time and eternity', but these photographic 'sites of remembrance', rather than being straightforward *aides memoire* that function to remind, recall and bring back to life, can actually block the
work of remembering.

Hirsch developed this concept of postmemory — a complicated concept, because of its problematic link with postmodernity
and its fragmentation — in relation to children of Shoah survivors, although she believes it can usefully describe other second
generation memories of cultural or collective traumatic events and
experiences. Postmemory is distinguished from memory by generational distance and from history by deep personal connection.
Postmemory is a powerful and very particular form of memory
precisely because its connection to its object or source is mediated
not through recollection but through an imaginative investment
and creation. This is not to say memory itself is unmediated, but
that it is more directly connected to the past. Postmemory charac-
terises the experience of those who grow up dominated by narratives that preceded their birth, whose own belated stories are
evacuated by the stories of the previous generation shamed by
traumatic events that can be neither understood nor recreated
(Hirsch, 1997, p. 22).

In 1984, guided by what I now understand as postmemory, or
a shadowy transferred memory, dominated by narratives that
preceded my birth, I began excavating the stories of members of
my mother's family who were exiled to Transnistria during the
Second World War when I journeyed to Bukovina to spend time
in Vatra Dornei, Mother's birthplace. There I met her school
friends, old Jews, the remnants of a once prosperous community,
who, when they returned from Transnistria after the war, stayed

in Bukovina, ageing, lonely and afraid. As that trip did not take me across the Dniester River into Transnistria itself, the book that resulted (Lentin, 1989) told the story of Transnistria only as a distant presence. A silence. When I was researching my doctorate, on Israeli daughters of Shoah survivors who are writers and film makers (Lentin, 2000), Transnistria returned to haunt me through the narratives of Nava Semel, whose parents came from Bukovina and whose father was involved in rescuing Transnistria's Jewish orphans at the end of the war, and of the film maker Orna Ben Dor, whose father spent his childhood in Transnistria.

This essay stems from my ongoing preoccupation with what has been termed the 'forgotten Holocaust'. More specifically, it deals with the experiences of women who were girls in that forgotten place, a forgotten place they cannot delete from their memory, as Transnistria survivor Sonia Palti writes:

> I should have forgotten it all! I should have forgotten the nightmare! But it was not possible. It is beyond my power to forget. During long sleepless nights, during warm afternoons when I just rest, the events that took place during my fourteen months of exile to Transnistria are constantly resurfacing in my mind like a movie (Palti, 1983, p. 11).

Although the focus on children began during the Shoah itself, and although many testimonies depicting the extent of the suffering of some 1.5 million children who perished in the ghettos, labour camps and extermination camps were collected in the ghettos and published immediately after the war, Dalia Ofer (2001) argues that research focusing specifically on children was not a central component of the social history of the Shoah. I have chosen to study girl survivors of Transnistria because of the relative silence until the 1980s about Transnistria in Shoah historiography and, until recently, about the gender aspect of Shoah historiography and testimony and, more specifically, because of the rarity of gender-specific accounts of child Shoah survivors.

I begin this essay with Transnistria itself — place, time, and some facts and figures. I then make some observations about silence: silence about the Shoah in general, and in the social sciences in particular; the specific silence about Transnistria; and the silence about the gendered implications of the Shoah. Then, using quotes from published memories and from interviews conducted with women survivors in Israel, I give voice to the experiences of women who were girls during the Shoah, experiences character-ised, above all, by the sheer chaos that was Transnistria. I conclude by posing some questions about the meanings, for twenty-first-century society, of breaking the silence about that 'forgotten ceme-tery' in relation to memory, postmemory, trauma and childhood, and in a postscript, end, as I began, with a personal reflection.

TRANSNISTRIA

Transnistria, a political unit created by the Nazis, was the name given to the 40,000 square kilometres between the River Dniester to the west, the River Bug to the east and the Black Sea to the South, in the southernmost corner of Ukraine (see Map 1). It ex-isted for two and a half years, from August 1941 to March 1944, when the Soviet Red Army liberated it. Transnistria — a term coined by Hitler himself — was given by Nazi Germany to Ro-mania after its conquest from the Soviets in order to compensate the Romanians, as Nazi allies, for Transylvania and southern Do-bruja which passed to Hungary and Bulgaria, and for Bukovina and Bessarabia, which were invaded by the Soviets and annexed to the USSR in June 1941. These regions were returned to Romania after the retreat of the Red Army (Ofer, 2000, p. 38). Interestingly, to the local Jewish population, forced to share accommodation and other scarce resources with the deported Jews, the term Transnistria was foreign. Tatyana Gutman, a native of Moghilev, which was to become one of the main Transnistria ghettos, who survived there during the war, observes:

> [T]o us, Ukrainian Jews, this was our home. We'd never heard of the name 'Transnistria' (Steigman-Carmelly, 1997, p. 257).

Map 1: Transnistria — The Territory between the Rivers Dniester and Bug

Source: Lavi (1960) in Steigman-Carmelly, 1997, p. 53.

Transnistria was a geographical freak, but a historic reality. Described as the 'largest killing field in the Holocaust', Transnistria was where half of Romania's pre-war Jewish population, mostly from Bessarabia and Bukovina, were deported. Between July 1941 and January 1942, some 125,000 Jews from Bessarabia and Bukovina, among them members of my own family, were deported to the region, followed, in 1942 and 1943, by some 5,000 others. They joined the 300,000 local Jews, most of whom were murdered by the SS and Einstazgruppen D (Ofer, 1999, pp. 176–7).

Because of the disorganisation and haphazard methods of destruction employed by the Romanians, the exact number of victims is not known. Researchers offer different (and sometimes contradictory) estimates. Ofer estimates that of the 300,000 Jews who lived in the region under the German-Romanian occupation, only 20,000 survived the war. But, she points out, the fact that there was no systematic annihilation plan resulted in 40 per cent of deportees surviving Transnistria (Ofer, 1999, p. 49). Unlike Nazi Germany, whose goal was the annihilation of Europe's Jews, Romania was concerned 'only' with deporting or killing the Jews in its own territory. In addition, Romania's 36,000 pre-war Roma population was also deported to Transnistria, where most perished (Steigman-Carmelly, 1997).

Exact figures for Romania's pre-war Jewish population are not available, though Berenbaum's (1997, p. xiii) claim that Romania's Jewish population of more than 750,000 was the third largest in Europe, after Russia and Poland, offers an indication of its dimensions.[3] Most Romanian Jews made a living as merchants, professionals, door-to-door salesmen, artisans, actors, musicians and craftsmen, but the fact that they included landowners and industrialists among their number ensured that they were the targets of economically motivated envy and hatred, though many also eked out an existence in typical east European shtetls (Steigman-Carmelly, 1997, p. 11). The accession to power of the fascist Iron Guard and the ensuing Citizenship Revision Law of January 1940, which deprived 200,000 Romanian Jews of citizenship (Ioanid, 1997, pp. 217–36), paved the way to scapegoating the Jews for the enforced ceding of Bessarabia and northern Bukovina to the Soviet Union.

Romanian antisemitism emerged as a powerful political force with the establishment, in the 1920s, of the Legion of the Archangel Saint Michael (also known as the Iron Guard and the All for the Country Party). In September 1940, General (later Marshall) Ion Antonescu set up, together with the Iron Guard, the National Legionary State. However, in January 1941, following an abortive rebellion against his rule, the Iron Guard was banned (*Antisemitism World Report*, 1996, p. 199), and Antonescu allowed the Nazis to take total control of Romania's economy. He also fully endorsed Nazi anti-Jewish policies and, late in 1941, his government dissolved the Federation of the Unions of Jewish Communities and replaced it with the Central Bureau for Jews.

---

[3] After the war about 400,000 Jews were left: about half of Romania's Jews were deported to Transnistria, of whom 50,000 came back (Steigman-Carmelly, 1997, p. xxiii). In 1996 the Jewish population numbered between 9,000 and 15,000 out of a total Romanian population of 23.3 million (*Antisemitism World Report*, 1996, p. 198).

The deportations to Transnistria were not only an expedient pro-Nazi policy, they were also a product of traditional Romanian antisemitism, fostered by nationalist intellectuals whose anti-semitism was nurtured by mythical anti-Jewish phobias as well as by so-called 'rational' ethnic and social anti-Jewish sentiments (Volovici, 2000, pp. 5–6). Lya Benjamin, who has examined the records of 1940–44 cabinet and ministerial council meetings, has highlighted the regime's complex and contradictory anti-Jewish policy, which included the confiscation of Jewish property, ethnic cleansing, deportation to Transnistria and Nazi death camps, dis-criminatory measures (such as the wearing of the distinctive mark, the ban on conversion, supply restrictions), and enforced emigration (Benjamin, 1997, pp. 3–18). Antisemitism was also cen-tral to Iron Guard doctrines:

> [T]he Jew was the mortal enemy of Romania because of his identification with the debased products of the west — anti-Christian communism as well as liberal democracy (Fischer-Galati, 1993, pp. 53–4).

Significantly, Jews were the third largest ethnic group in the bud-ding Romanian Communist Party; at 18.2 per cent, their member-ship was substantially above their proportion (4 per cent) of the general population (Shafir, 1985, pp. 25–6).

Between July 1940 and August 1941, and prior to the mass de-portations to Transnistria, several pogroms were pursued with the utmost cruelty by government forces, the Iron Guard and the local populations in Dorohoi, Bucharest, Iasi, Edinets, Beltz and Kishinev. The Iasi pogrom resulted in 8,000 to 10,000 Jewish vic-tims, some of whom died in the 'death trains' that travelled slowly and aimlessly from one station to another. Packed into air-less containers, Jews died of thirst, infection and heat (Dawid-owicz, 1975, p. 461; Steigman-Carmelly, 1997, pp. 22–50). Even the Nazis believed the Romanians were unnecessarily cruel. In his report on the Iasi pogrom, Italian journalist Curzio Malaparte de-scribed a conversation between Frank, the Nazi governor-general of Poland, and Fischer, the governor of Warsaw, during which

Frank observed that 'the Romanian people are not a civilised people' (Steigman-Carmelly, 1997, p. xxiii).

The deportations to Transnistria began in September 1941. Transnistria consisted of some 132 Ukrainian towns and villages, many of which became concentration, transit and labour camps. Survivor and author Ruth Glassberg-Gold describes the first chaotic hours of the deportations:

> November 1941. . . . That morning the soldiers banged on our door, cursing and swearing. They ordered us to leave the apartment. Carrying rucksacks and a few packed things we left our house forever. Terrified, I looked silently at the chaos on the streets, familiar to me since childhood and hitherto peaceful. There were hordes of people, shoving and pushing mercilessly. . . . Before we could collect ourselves, we were swallowed in that chaotic deportation — people of all ages and classes, women holding screaming babies in their arms, sick people supported by children, old people bent under their belongings . . . (Glassberg-Gold, 1999, p. 63).

The Romanians established several points along the River Dniester where Jews were ordered to cross the river by bridge or on overcrowded barges and rafts. The crossings and the ensuing human convoys were overseen by Romanian soldiers, who shot Jews unable to keep pace because of weakness or illness. They were also ordered to dig a pit every ten kilometres capable of containing the bodies of up to 100 Jews who were unable to proceed. Deportees who died on those death convoys were also left on the side of the road. People died from exhaustion, cold, hunger and illness before they reached the camps. Some, having exchanged their clothes for food, walked naked in temperatures of up to 40 degrees below zero (Ancel, 1997; Steigman-Carmelly, 1997). Ruth Glassberg-Gold describes the death convoys from a child's point of view:

> As we were advancing (on our death march) I noticed a strange thing: on both sides of the road I saw tree stumps

covered in snow, which looked like human figures. Confused, I tried to understand what they were, but from the cart I could not decipher them. . . . I asked the adults for an explanation, but they hesitated. Only when I insisted they told me the shocking truth — these were swollen, frozen human bodies from previous deportations, people who were unable to stand the march and stayed to die by the side of the road forever. . . . [The bodies] were everywhere — in the barns, the cellars and inside the houses . . . they were abandoned like animals, nobody bothered to close their glassy eyes, which seemed to be imploring for rest (Ruth Glassberg-Gold, 1999, pp. 75–6).

Martha Ellenbogen, another woman survivor, links accounts of death with more private memories of girlhood when she speaks of the convoys:

One place shocked me. Obadovka. I will never forgive myself. People died at the side of the road. It was the end of October. For the first time in my life I saw frozen people in the ditches by the side of the road. I was very scared. I won't forgive myself for having made life difficult for my mother, because I didn't want to go to sleep. She didn't know what to do. . . . They opened the door and we saw naked people, thin as skeletons . . .

Survivors tell of Romanian Jewish deportees being housed in cowsheds, pigsties, chicken coops, or in the already overcrowded houses of local Ukrainian Jews. Overcrowding resulted in lice infestations that caused typhus, which killed both deportees and local Transnistrian Jews.

SILENCE: WHY TRANSNISTRIA? WHY NOW?

Asking why Transnistria, why now, and why girlhood, leads me first to the discussion of the multifaceted and contradictory role silence plays in our attempt to make a degree of sense of the Shoah. It is perhaps absurd to speak of silence in relation to the Shoah, a topic about which a huge number of memoirs, scholarly books, research projects, and survivor testimony projects as well as works of fiction, poetry, films and other works of art have been produced. There is an ongoing debate about the appropriateness of speech about the Shoah, inspired by Adorno's famous dictum about the impossibility of writing poems after Auschwitz (Adorno, 1949). While some say that silence is the only appropriate response, others — myself included — argue that silence would be a surrender to cynicism and, by implication, to the very forces that created Auschwitz in the first place. Although silences about the Shoah are themselves conveyed through language, a degree of silence about the Shoah continues.

Zygmunt Bauman (1989) argues that there has been a tendency, until recently, to present the Shoah as an exclusively Jewish tragedy, thus marginalizing it. This ignores the fact that other populations — Roma, homosexual men, political prisoners and prisoners of war — were also targeted by the Nazis. Alternatively, writers and researchers tend to present the annihilation as primeval or as a 'natural' predisposition of 'human nature', thus making it a-historical and un-researchable. Bauman makes a strong case for theorising the Shoah as an outcome of *modernity*, when modernising instruments such as rationality, technology and bureaucracy were harnessed to state violence. He reminds us that

> the Holocaust, born and executed in our modern rational society, at the high stage of our civilisation and at the peak of human achievement . . . is a problem of that society, civilisation and culture (Bauman, 1989, p. x).

In the state of Israel — the destination for many survivors and where all my interviewees live — the Shoah was a silenced presence for many years. On the one hand, the survivors were tutored in self-silencing. Israeli writer Aharon Appelfeld, who survived as a child in Transnistria's ghettos and in the forest, says this about breaking the silence in his writings:

> My first written words were sort of desperate attempts to find the silence that surrounded me during the war and to

return me to myself. With my blind senses I understood
that within this silence rests my soul (Appelfeld, 1999, pp.
95–6).

On the other hand, however, Israel — intent on constructing itself
as the antithesis to the supposedly weak and passive European
diaspora that had allegedly gone to its death 'like lambs to the
slaughter' — did not offer survivors a forum to relate their experiences. Struggling for survival and privileging 'national security',
Israeli state and society set out publicly to commemorate the
Shoah and privilege the sporadic acts of armed resistance by the
few over the victimhood of the millions (Segev, 1991; Lentin, 2000).

This silence about Jewish victimhood during the Shoah has
been lifting gradually since the mid-1980s. It has been argued that
it takes a generation — the survivors getting older and their
grandchildren beginning to ask — for a traumatised society to begin to confront its traumatic past. However, even as the veil of
silence began lifting elsewhere, Transnistria remained shrouded
in silence in the eyes of its survivors. According to Felicia Steigman-Carmelly, this 'blatant, but unintentional neglect is an additional source of pain in the web of trauma' (Steigman-Carmelly,
1997, p. xix). The reasons for this silence have to do with the un-
availability of archival material from the former Soviet bloc until
recent years; with the refusal of Romania to accept responsibility
for its wartime crimes (Steigman-Carmelly, 1997, p. xxiv); and
with the survivors themselves.

On the Romanian side there was active Holocaust denial (*Antisemitism World Report*, 1996, p. 203). Communist and postcommunist Romania waged a 'history-cleansing' campaign in order to convince the Romanian people and the world that there
was no holocaust in their country (Braham, 1997). This resulted,
for instance, in a secret deal between Romania's communist dicta-
tor Nicolae Ceausescu and Israel, making Romania the only Iron
Curtain state to allow Jewish immigration to Israel — at a price.
Holocaust denial involved active efforts to rehabilitate Antonescu,
who collaborated with the Nazis, but who also responded to ap-

peals from the then chief rabbi, Alexadre Safran, and leading Romanians from the Queen Mother downwards by refusing to deport the Jews of the Romanian *Regat*. He also gave shelter to Jews who escaped from north Transylvania. Thus independent Romania became one of the few safe havens for Jews in occupied Europe (Gallagher, 1995, p. 47). Indeed, party-supported 'official historians' undertook

> to portray Antonescu's Romania as a country that not only prevented the Holocaust, but also afforded a haven to thousands of foreign Jews and allowed their emigration to Palestine (Braham, 1997, p. 49; see also Eskenasy, 1997; Shafir, 1997).

The campaign to rehabilitate Antonescu is ongoing. In 1991 Romania's President Illiescu, opposing extreme right antisemitism, rejected growing pressure to rehabilitate Antonescu by Romanians seeking a strong ruler who would sweep away internal tensions, put an end to foreign meddling and make Romania 'great again'. He declared that he 'did not share the opinion of those who wished to rehabilitate him, keeping silent on the negative aspects of his activity', and described Antonescu as 'Hitler's ally [who] pushed the country into war' (Gallagher, 1995, p. 115).

From the point of view of the Transnistria survivors, the prominence afforded the Nazi extermination camps in the history of the Shoah served to discourage them from assuming the survivor mantle. Their losses, which numbered only a few hundred thousand, and were attributable to the combined impact of disease, hunger, cold and sporadic killings did not, it seemed, deserve to be compared with the millions exterminated in the Nazi death camps (although, as I show below, some survivors understand this comparison differently). Thus, Israeli Transnistria survivors were often embarrassed to speak of their ordeal in the shadow of Auschwitz. The 100,000 Romanian Jews who came to Israel between 1948 and 1949 were busy trying to integrate and were reluctant to speak of their ordeal, of which no one in the young state wanted to hear (personal communication, Tel Aviv,

March 2000). This is borne out by the words of women survivors I
have interviewed. Thus Martha Ellenbogen observes:

> To this day I have not given testimony in *Yad Vashem*. It's
> difficult. I can understand that people did not believe us . . .

Likewise Bertha Abrahami:

> No one asked us anything. . . . Nor was I interested in
> telling. Because no one can transmit the feelings . . .

In Mark Simyonovics's film *Transnistria, the Hell*, survivors speak
with great pain about the silencing. Shmuel Ben Zion, who has
written about Jewish children in Transnistria, observes:

> I have been in Israel for 22 years. No one knew about our
> Holocaust, I never heard a word about it . . .

Sonia Palti concurs:

> When I returned after 14 months exile in Transnistria, I
> wanted to tell my friends about the extermination, about
> torture, about hunger, about beatings, about exile, to tell
> what Transnistria was for us. I realised that no one wanted
> to hear. So as a child of 15 I had a strange experience: I
> understood I had to keep quiet (Simyonovics, 1999).

Indeed, apart from a few studies and memoirs, which began appearing in the 1980s, Transnistria remained largely unacknowledged until Simyonovics's three programmes broadcast on Israeli Educational Television in 1999 put the spotlight on this
dark corner.

Gender is another silence in relation to the Shoah. Studies of
the gendered meanings of the Nazi genocide and the gendered
experiences of women began appearing only in the early 1980s.
Joan Ringelheim, a pioneer in this area, argues that women's experiences should be studied separately since women's experiences
were different from men's experiences; one example was
women's vulnerability to specific sexual exploitation. However,

researching the sexual abuse of women during the Shoah is extremely difficult, since it raises the possibility that mothers, sisters, or lovers traded their sexuality for survival, and confronts relatives, but also researchers, with our own sexual vulnerability (Ringelheim, 1997, p. 25). That said, accounts of the pre-deportation Romanian pogroms attest to the widespread rape of women and girls. During the Kishinev pogrom, while male Jews were captured as slave labour, women were

> dragged to satisfy the sexual lust of the [Romanian] 'liberators'. On August 1, 1941, 450 Jews were pulled out of the ghetto, mostly intellectuals and beautiful women. . . . Some of the surviving women and girls were transported to the Soroca military brothel (Steigman-Carmelly, 1997, p. 49).

Finally, why child survivors? With 50 per cent of the deportees to Transnistria being children — many of whom lost their parents during the first winter to cold, typhus and dysentery — and unlike Nazi concentration camps, where being a child was reason for immediate gassing, a relatively high proportion of Transnistria survivors were children. Survivors insist that Transnistria was different because of the large proportion of child survivors. According to Martha Ellenbogen,

> [C]hildren survived in greater numbers than adults; it must
> be because of their greater resilience and physical reserves.

Steigman-Carmelly (1997, p. 119) writes of thousands of children roaming the muddy roads from camp to camp. Many were separated from their parents. Many, having witnessed the death or murder of their parents, eventually joined groups of wandering children, looking or begging for shelter and food. Many were unable to say what happened to them or their families. For some orphans, begging was the only way to survive. For others, it was shameful, as Klara Ostfeld, whose mother was so weak with typhus that 'she had to hold on to building walls while she walked', writes:

> I was nine years old, one gloomy afternoon, when I left the
> room I shared with so many others. Without telling
> anybody I went out into the street. I wandered about the
> narrow depressing roads of the Moghilev ghetto. I saw
> other children my age wrapped in rags with newspapers
> around their feet. . . . I found myself in the market. There
> were long benches piled high with enticing foods. . . . My
> mouth was watering at the sight of these foods. . . . I stared
> at them as my thoughts were wandering back into my life
> before deportation. A voice rudely shocked me out of my
> reverie, 'Aren't you ashamed to beg?' I was flooded with
> shame. . . . When I left the market I no longer felt hunger,
> just shame and a deep emptiness (Ostfeld in Steigman-
> Carmelly, 1997, pp. 305–6).

Refusing to take part in begging with the other children in the orphanage was a way of preserving Ruth Glassberg-Gold's indi-
viduality:

> After they denuded me of my individuality and my
> identity, I forced myself to . . . keep the link with my past,
> with my being Ruthie. I observed basic behaviour rules
> imparted by my parents, and which my mother repeated
> on her deathbed. For instance, I refused to take part in the
> routine kept by the other children, which included begging
> or stealing food (Glassberg-Gold, 1999, p. 120).

One of the main Jewish resistance strategies was the establishment of orphanages for these abandoned children. Dora Litani
(1981) lists ten orphanages, the first set up in Moghilev in April
1942. The orphanages were supported by the Jewish community
of the Old Romanian Kingdom, many of whose members survived the war under the King and Antonescu, intent on protecting
'their own' Jews. In 1943, a Jewish commission from Romania visited Transnistria. After Soviet advances on the eastern front, the
Romanian government, working towards a separate peace agreement with the Allies, agreed to the return of 5,000 out of the surviving 8,000 orphans, albeit only those under 15 who had lost

both parents. The Romanians were prepared to assist with their immigration to Palestine, in return for a large sum of money. However, by the end of 1944 only 1,105 orphans from Transnistria had reached Palestine. Yitzhak Arzi, a member of the team sent to rescue the orphans, says this about the Moghilev orphanage he visited in February 1944:

> The windowless building was horrifyingly cold. I felt as if I had arrived at Dante's Inferno. Legless and armless children lay on the ramshackle beds; their limbs had frozen during their wanderings in the winter of 1941–2. They were covered in rags and torn blankets, their faces were ashen and hunger filled their eyes. For lunch they got a bowl of soup and a slice of bread. A heavy stench filled the air. I walked between the beds, staring at the pale faces and the emaciated bodies. These pictures will be with me for the rest of my life. I managed to penetrate their apathy only when I told them I came to take them out of this place and bring them to Erez Israel. Their eyes lit up. Some jumped out of their beds . . . but others were completely unresponsive (Arzi, 1999, p. 95).

In this essay I concentrate on women survivors whose accounts intersect with my family history. In written and oral testimonies, the women depict their girlhood against the richly textured, often privileged life of Bukovina's Jews, who were the commercial and cultural German-speaking élite in this region of the Carpathians (Map 2). They all focus on the rupture of childhood and emphasise the unique depravity of the Transnistria experience in the annals of the Holocaust. Attempting to categorise the testimonies of Auschwitz survivors along gender lines, sociologist Mary Lagerwey (1998) has concluded that they were 'too complex to fit neatly into gender categories' and that ultimately what she initially thought of as 'gendered narratives', were narratives of *chaos* (1998, p. 127). Indeed, chaos is one recurring theme in the accounts of Transnistria survivors.

*Map 2: Province of Bucovina with Jewish Population Prior to
World War II*

Source: Gilbert, 1993, p. 72, cited in Steigman-Carmelly, 1997, p. 53.

Implemented by less technological means than in Nazi-controlled
territories, and unlike the Nazi annihilation plan which was systematically organised, where arguably death was for the most
part quick and 'sanitary', the Romanian methods were barbaric.
According to Aharon Appelfeld:

> [T]hey used old-fashioned methods, not as in Auschwitz.
> This meant long and extended deaths, hunger, cold, illness.
> Or they would take people out and simply shoot them. But
> they saved bullets. They didn't shoot the children, they
> simply threw them out (Simyonovics, 1999).

However, there was a broad consensus in Romania, from the highest state officials down to the most humble civil servant in village offices, that the Jews had to be killed or deported. This campaign was carried out in Romania before the extermination camps began to function elsewhere in Europe. Ofer (2000, p. 39) argues that the history of Transnistria, despite its uniqueness, can be studied as a mini-history of the Holocaust. Yet according to Matatias Carp in *Cartea Neagra (the Black Book*, 1946–48, cited in Steigman-Carmelly, 1997), the Iasi pogrom, despite 'predicting the future massacres which were to annihilate six million Jews in the following three years', remained unspoken at the time and for a long period afterwards.

Despite the chaos experienced by the survivors I have interviewed, all of whom were very young girls at the time, new archival materials demonstrate that the Romanians employed their own rationale for deportation. This embraced fear of the widespread typhus epidemic of the 1941–2 winter, and the need to supply slave labour to build the Nazi Poland-Ukraine highway which accounts for the Trans-Bug Nazi-controlled labour camps modelled on the Nazi camps in Poland. These materials also demonstrate a clear command structure on the Romanian side. This has led Steigman-Carmelly to conclude that 'while chaos and disorganisation otherwise prevailed, the persecution and extermination of the targeted Jewish population was executed with cruel determination', so much so that by May 1942, a few months after the deportations began, almost two-thirds of Transnistria's Jews were dead (Steigman-Carmelly, 1997, p. 89).

However, Transnistria is also characterised by successful Jewish resistance strategies. According to Ofer, the absence of a systematic annihilation plan, combined with disorganisation and the susceptibility of Romanian officials to bribery, enabled the Jewish leadership to formulate strategies of assistance and relief from the spring of 1942. Despite its lateness and inadequacy, the relief contributed to survival: 'no other Jewish community in Nazi Europe received such massive assistance' (Ofer, 2000, p. 39).

The Narratives: Ruptured Childhood

> When I lay on the ground a week after I witnessed my
> mother's death, hungry, broken, alone, an orphan, between
> strangers, I thought, if I remain alive I will tell the whole
> world what I experienced. And no one will believe me
> (Esther Gelbelman in Simyonovics, 1999).

All the narratives — written and oral — begin with descriptions
of the idyllic, protected childhoods of the pampered daughters of
the Jewish bourgeoisie who, particularly in pre-war Bukovina,
had both the economic and cultural freedom to lead a well-off, yet
traditional Jewish existence. As a narrative device, this highlights
the sharp rupture that was to come. Most of the narrators were
nine to eleven years old at the outbreak of war. The changing relations with the local population, seeing parents being humiliated
by neighbours and customers who had joined the Iron Guard,
were the first signs of the chaos to come. Ruth Glassberg-Gold,
who grew up in Milie, a picturesque village outside Czernowitz,
describes her shock at hearing that the Jewish population of Milie
was massacred by its neighbours after she and her family had fled
to Czernowitz:

> The carrier of the appalling news was my mother's cousin.
> . . . He managed to shout in a choked voice towards (our)
> fourth-floor window: 'Anna! Anna! They have all been
> murdered!' Later, when we found out that all our friends
> and relatives had been murdered, not by the soldiers but by
> their neighbours with whom they had lived in harmony,
> our panic increased (Glassberg-Gold, 1999, p. 54).

The deportations signalled the real rupture of childhood, as
Felicia Steigman-Carmelly writes:

> Having been a sheltered child, the only granddaughter to
> my grandparents . . . I was very naïve, pampered and
> completely unprepared for the perils facing me. After
> surviving the forced abandonment of my home and

birthplace and the atrocious deportation train, I no longer felt like a child. My childhood was denied to me, it was robbed by evil people who had complete power over our lives . . . (Steigman-Carmelly, 1997, p. 233).

Several themes unite all the narratives: the rupture of previously privileged childhoods; having to witness the death of loved ones; being faced with epidemics and death for the first time; having to part with prized childhood possessions; having to exist, flea-ridden and terrified of the typhus epidemic; being forcibly shaved and deprived of their budding femininity; employing complex barter systems and other resistance strategies; and, finally, having to live with memories that most have suppressed for many years.

The narrators' accounts of the deportations proper are recalled with confusion and a degree of revulsion. The packed trains and lack of hygiene signal another rupture with the narrators' bourgeois upbringing and warm family relations that feature prominently:

> They sent us in cattle trains to Bessarabia; Merkulesti, the last stop. A border station between Russia and Romania. . . . It was there that I got the shock of my life. It was there I think that we lost our humanity. We got off the train, there were soldiers, Romanians, Germans, dogs; and they all relieved themselves outside the train, without shame. We simply got off the train . . . men, women, children, everyone together. This is a picture I shall never forget (Bertha Abrahami).

Some deportees were housed in pigsties, stables or cowsheds — sometimes with up to 1,500 strangers to a shed. As Martha Ellenbogen relates:

> We arrived in Potshana, and were put in a cowshed. There were troughs on both sides . . . the cows were no longer there, we lived there instead of the cows. We lay side by side, improvising with blankets, coats and straw. We

stayed there with strangers, people we had never met before.

Others were lodged in the houses of local Ukrainian Jews, many of whom were reluctant to allow them in, as Ruth Glassberg-Gold explains:

> When our convoy entered the narrow snow-covered streets, we all tried to find shelter with the few remaining local Jews. A multitude of exhausted and emaciated humans knocked on doors looking for shelter. The first, and the wealthiest, got the best houses. We too knocked on many doors, but I do not remember seeing any human form. I can only remember the word 'typh' meaning typhus, shouted at us from behind closed doors. The local Jews clearly used this excuse in order to chase us away. We had no option but to locate in the back room of a partially ruined house (Glassberg-Gold, 1999, p. 84).

Narrators stress the difference between the accounts of children who survived the war with their families and those who survived alone. Martha Ellenbogen's endured the latter experience:

> Father was sent to Russia and we were deported with Mother . . . . When Mother died, I remained completely alone.

Having become immune to the pain, survivors often tell of the death of loved relatives almost flatly, recounting death as a 'natural' consequence of the horrors. They speak with particular pain about the death of mothers, as illustrated by Martha Ellenbogen:

> In the stable people became ill and began to die. Those who died were placed in the aisle and the bodies were stacked up until the carts arrived. . . . Meanwhile my mother became ill with typhus. This couple we befriended came and saw she was dying and said that if anything happened to Mother, I should say nothing and they would come to see us in the morning . . . they were afraid that if the others

saw that she had died, they would take away my few remaining things. I lay beside Mother and warmed her with my body . . . in the morning they came, and Mother was no longer alive.

Bertha Abrahami:

We walked on, and my mother became ill. Very ill. And died.

And Ruth Glassberg-Gold:

After fourteen sleepless nights, I was defeated by sleep. But a sense of duty chased me in my dreams. I woke up and shook her, 'Mother, Mother!' Silence. I shook her a little more, but she did not respond with her usual weak 'hmmm'. She used the fact that I had fallen asleep and could not interrupt her dying silently and fleeing that crazy world (Glassberg-Gold, 1999, pp. 98–9).

The prevalence of death meant that narrators were often unsure as to their own continuing existence, as Bertha Abrahami testifies:

We walked and walked and arrived somewhere, a sort of former Kolkhoz. . . . On the way there I had already had fever . . . we were no longer clean. I remember Father held me in his arms and there was a table, and Father asked the people to allow him to put the child on the table because she had fever. I lay on the table and I remember thinking that we were in a train, or something, I don't know. Every morning they got the dead out. I remember that I didn't know whether I was alive or dead, if they were taking me out or not.

Rosa Ruth Zuckermann's recollection contains similar echoes:

How did they die? I was in a daze, I also had typhus. I thought that in the end it would be my turn to die. I never thought I'd survive. For many years I was ashamed I was still alive . . . (Simyonovics, 1999).

Narrators also tell of recovering from illness, sometimes against all the odds. Take Martha Ellenbogen's experience:

> [After Mother's death], the couple we met took me to where they lived. But when I arrived I was sick myself. In the midst of all that hell, they could have left me where I was, but they took me with them when I was already ill. The landlady was not to know I was there. . . . I was delirious and spoke out of fever. And it lasted a long time, a whole month. I had no energy. I received no medicine. And all the time I dreamt my father was coming with a box of chocolates. I suppose children's immune system is really stronger . . .

SURVIVAL STRATEGIES

Deportees improvised various strategies of survival, which included selling valuables, bartering with the local Ukrainian peasants, knitting, collecting and selling scraps of timber. Bartering was a common survival strategy. Martha Ellenbogen relates:

> As soon as we arrived, the villagers approached and we began a process of *zaminai* — barter. We bought anything we could buy in exchange for our clothes, although doing this was not a good thing as it became very cold.

Ruth Glassberg-Gold learnt a bitter lesson about the value of things:

> Although we lived side by side with the dead, we were still alive and we needed food and water. In our hardship we invented various tricks, including a unique barter system. . . . A blouse was worth an onion, a coat a loaf of bread, and so on. Naturally people who had more valuable things, jewellery for instance, could do better deals and this gave them a better chance of survival. These were hard lessons in the facts of life (Glassberg-Gold, 1999, p. 76).

Valuables often meant the difference between eating and starving. The narrators recall parting with precious childhood possessions. Martha Ellenbogen recounts:

> Before we left Merculesti, we were told to give up our valuables. . . . I had a pair of earrings with little round stones . . . . Mother wanted me to remove them, but I didn't agree. I covered them with my braids and the earrings became important . . . later it transpired that I would have to part with my earrings. I got 16 kilograms of cornmeal for them and we ate one or two spoonfuls of *mamaliga*. Since then I can't even hear of *mamaliga*. We were always hungry. And since that time I have never worn earrings . . .

But sometimes valuables were robbed, as Felicia Steigman-Carmelly remembers:

> Now we are on the other side of the Dniester. Again, screaming, swearing, cursing and shoving from the soldiers. A soldier jerks out one of my earrings and blood is running from my ear (1997, p. 232).

There were other survival strategies. Martha Ellenbogen, who was deported to Bershad, collected small pieces of timber from the sawmills where some deportees worked:

> [W]e walked seven kilometres at night carrying the sticks on our backs. At dawn we sold the sticks and then walked seven kilometres back. Of course people did not pay us, but gave us a little bread, a little flour, a few potatoes or potato peels.

Other children knitted for the locals, as Felicia Steigman-Carmelly recounts:

> [W]hen we had nothing left to barter, we started knitting scarves, gloves, socks and sweaters in exchange for some potatoes, beets, corn flour or beans. . . . The wool was so rough that after a few minutes of knitting, our fingers

would bleed. But we couldn't stop knitting, because we
needed the food (1997, p. 235).

As a way of fighting the typhus epidemic, girls were often shaved
bald to arrest lice infestation. They recall being deprived of their
budding femininity with great pain. Ruth Glassberg-Gold was glad
when her long braids were cut off, but when told she would have
to shave her hair completely in order to stop the lice infestation:

> I looked desperately at my beautiful hair falling on the
> ground and felt naked and ashamed. I was hurt not only
> because I was no longer beautiful, but because I no longer
> looked like a girl. My identity was robbed and I felt
> humiliated. My only consolation was that older girls too
> had to bear this humiliation, and after our heads were
> shaved we all looked alike, women and men, strange,
> grotesque (Glassberg-Gold, 1999, pp. 77–8).

DEEP MEMORY, COMMON MEMORY

The narrative strategies employed by the women survivors of
Transnistria embrace chronicity; ruptured idyllic childhoods;
comparisons with other Shoah experiences, particularly in relation to the chaos that was Transnistria; and evaluations that locate
the inner, personal memories of the Transnistria experience
within a broader understanding of Shoah, memory and post
Shoah. According to Aharon Appelfeld, child survivors retell the
Shoah differently from adults:

> Children lack chronology. I don't remember names of places.
> I only remember colours and sounds. On the one hand, it is a
> childhood trauma, and on the other, he is a child. . . . I
> remember the suffering, of course, but because we were
> children we would also play, between death and death,
> between hunger and hunger, a child is a child. Therefore we
> absorbed it as a totality while for adults it was an episode.
> For children it was not an episode, it was our childhood.
> When children began to tell, they did not write memoirs,

they used art. All the people who tried to describe the Shoah using art were children during the Shoah, which they captured through art (Simyonovics, 1999).

Charlotte Delbo's *Auschwitz and After* is an example of a multi-genre, non-linear Shoah memoir. Delbo, a French non-Jewish survivor of Auschwitz, wrote:

> Auschwitz is so deeply etched on my memory that I cannot forget one moment of it. So you are living with Auschwitz? No, I live next to it. Auschwitz is there, unalterable, precise, but enveloped in the skin of memory, an impermeable skin that isolates it from my present self (Delbo, 1995, p. xi).

Theorising the inability of Shoah survivors to proceed from past to present, Lawrence Langer developed the notion of 'common memory' as opposed to 'deep memory'. Common memory 'urges us to regard the Auschwitz ordeal as part of a chronology, [freeing] us from the pain of remembering the unthinkable'. Deep memory 'reminds us that the Auschwitz past is not really past and never will be' (Langer, 1991, p. xi). Delbo evokes painfully this rupture between Shoah past and the present: 'I have the feeling', she observes

> that the 'self' who was in the camp wasn't me, isn't the person who is here, opposite you. . . . And everything that happened to this other 'self', the one from Auschwitz, doesn't touch me now, doesn't concern me, so distinct are deep memory and common memory (Delbo, 1995, p. 13).

For the women who survived Transnistria as girls, whose childhood was so cruelly ruptured, later memories of rescue and redemption, in the state of Israel or elsewhere, were the common memory covering up the deep memory of the girls they had once been, whose past Transnistrian 'selves' are not really past and never will be. I would also suggest that the narratives of the women who survived Transnistria, precisely because of the multi-layered silences governing that 'forgotten Holocaust', and because of the breaking of that silence, can be understood as counter-narratives, bringing the Transnistria story into public consciousness. In my book on Israeli daughters of Shoah survivors (Lentin, 2000), I argue that their narratives often deviate from the linear Shoah narrative, the trajectory of which tends to begin prior to the Shoah, and continue via Shoah (and often *gevurah* — or acts of heroic resistance) to *tekumah* (redemption) in the state of Israel.[4] While the narratives I cite in this essay have a certain linear chronicity, they can also be read, precisely because of the long silence about Transnistria, as deviant counter-narratives, disrupting, after many mute years, the linearity of Israeli Shoah narratives.[5]

Historian and survivor Leon Volovici makes their claim to be heard most eloquently:

> These victims also deserve to be remembered, they also deserve a stone in *Yad Vashem* commemorating their annihilation. We want to come to *Yad Vashem* to remember and lay flowers, we want an inscription to commemorate the biggest camp (Simyonovics, 1999).

This is important, because in contemporary Transnistria there are no signs of the destruction, and no memorials. In the towns and villages of Bukovina — once flourishing cultural and commercial Jewish centres — there remain only handfuls of old Jews, not enough for prayer quorums. In Transnistria itself, the few remaining local Jews are isolated and fearful and the beautiful landscape does not reveal evidence of the massacre that took place. As Nava Semel, who narrated one of Simyonovics's films, says:

> [U]nder this beautiful cloak lies horror and suffering. What a terrible conflict, how does nature cover up the horrors underneath. After a few days here I became suspicious of

---

[4] One such example of a linear Transnistria memoir is Rita Sand-Landau's third-person memoir *The River Water Went Red . . .* (1992).

[5] See Lentin, 2001 for a discussion of second-generation Shoah narratives as gendered counter-narratives.

the landscape, I understood what it was hiding (Simyonovics, 1999).

In the current climate of women asylum-seekers having to cope with gendered torture as part of their asylum and integration processes in Europe, the accounts of women who survived as girls in Transnistria may help to shed light on the impossibility of forgetting childhood trauma and on the price of survival. Langer warns against the tendency to employ terms such as 'redeeming' and 'salvation' when working with Shoah testimonies. Having watched hundreds of video-recorded survivor testimonies, he concludes that, ultimately, Shoah testimonies are united by the 'unintended, unexpected, but invariably unavoidable failure' to link survivors' Shoah experiences with the rest of their lives (Langer, 1991, pp. 2–3). Shoah survival, according to Bauman (2000), is often valorised at the expense of morality; take, for instance, the title change of Thomas Keneally's novel from *Schindler's Ark* to *Schindler's List* in Spielberg's film — the former (like Noah's ark) — aiming to save all the species, the latter indicating a finite quality of saving some at the expense of others.

Often breaking the silence about Transnistria for the first time — even in the current climate of television confessions and video Shoah testimonies — the narratives of these girl survivors tell of confusion, lack of information, precariousness, and of Jews being prey to Nazis, Romanians and local Ukrainians on whose goodwill they depended for food and shelter. Seen from the point of view of these girls, who often looked after younger children or ailing parents, these chaotic narratives, far from denoting, as some would argue, 'the victory of the human spirit against all odds', tell only of rupture and death.

Concluding that the only way of categorising Auschwitz narratives is through the prism of chaos, Mary Lagerwey suggests that

> the chaos of Auschwitz overwhelms and twists individual existence into grotesque caricatures . . . stories of Auschwitz tell of the world of totalitarian domination,

where 'everything is possible'. In the tumult of Auschwitz and in the stories of its survivors, simple notions of multiple stories are overwhelmed by a cacophony of voices resonating with the bureaucratic violence that formed the essence of Auschwitz . . . it is a world of the bizarre, the incongruous, and the irrational (Lagerwey, 1995, p. 17).

However, while chaos may be the only way of refracting Auschwitz testimonies beyond categories of gender, class, and ethnic or national origin, Transnistria is remembered by its survivors as even more chaotic than Auschwitz, if that be possible. In the words of Martha Ellenbogen:

Transnistria was an awful thing. . . . Hungry every day. There were no clothes. No one wanted to know about me. I was only a little girl. . . . Everyone speaks about Auschwitz, but we were starved, we were sick, we had typhus, I never got medicines. I don't understand how I survived it.

Bertha Abrahami's recollection is similar:

No one gave us anything. You know, the Germans. . . . My husband was in Auschwitz. And yes, they killed, yes, they burned the people, but they gave them something small to eat, something, a bowl of soup. Here there was nothing. Total chaos.

CONCLUSION: POSTMEMORY?

I would like to end where I began, at the intersection of the personal and the collective. Postmemory, according to Marianne Hirsch, is not 'absent memory' or 'hole of memory'. Postmemory, often obsessive and relentless, need not be absent or evacuated; 'it is as full or as empty, certainly as constructed, as memory itself' (Hirsch, 1997, p. 22). As I was working with the accounts of women survivors of Transnistria I encountered many personal landmarks. Family photographs are the medium connecting first and second-generation remembrance, memory and postmemory.

Yet the presence of photographs lies not in their evocation of memory and the connection they can establish between past and present, but in their role as fragments of a history we cannot assimilate (Hirsch, 1992, p. 40).

My mother's family, the Schiebers — a respected, wealthy Bukovina family — was mentioned several times by my interviewees. I have few photographs to remember them by, but one particular story overwhelmed me. Most of the narrators told about people who helped them and rescued them from further jeopardy, often from death, once their parents were no longer alive. Ruth Glassberg-Gold tells of a couple she calls Mr and Mrs Sattinger, who cared for her after her mother's death. Glassberg-Gold describes Mrs Sattinger as 'not particularly friendly, perhaps because of her lameness', and her husband Marcus, as 'nicer, but not necessarily warm'. Even after the death of their own little girl, the Sattingers fulfilled the promise they made to Ruth's mother and found Ruth a home and eventually brought her to an orphanage, and thus saved her life. To my amazement, Mrs Sattinger turned out to be my mother's lame Aunt Rebecca, who moved from Transnistria to Israel in the 1950s, having lost her daughter and husband, with her only son, who was to die in the early 1990s, filling his mother's cup of sorrows. I remember Aunt Rebecca as a passive, rather depressed woman, who ended life in a home for the elderly, barely recognising my mother, her only remaining niece. The one photograph Mother had of Rebecca as a reasonably young woman shows a plump matriarch, dressed for the family wedding where the photograph was taken. Her hair had been carefully done, her dress, probably sewn by herself — she was a professional seamstress — and her necklace, reflect her loneliness, her bitterness. However, the photograph tells me nothing about her life, it does not help me remember her.

Figure 1: Rebecca Sattinger

I ended *Night Train to Mother*, my novel about Bukovina, with a
chapter about Hetti, based on Aunt Rebecca — an unconscious
gesture of postmemory. I would like to think that in that book I
found a key to Rebecca's life, but who knows? I end with 'my'
Hetti-Rebecca musing aloud about Transnistria, about her dead
husband, killed on a labour detail in a Transnistria forest, and
about the indelibility of deep memory:

> Sometimes in the early morning, when she cannot sleep,
> Hetti imagines Menashe hadn't died. That he is alive
> somewhere in Russia or Romania with another family. That
> he was told that it was she who died. But it makes no
> difference which of them died. And so she continues to live
> with his fading features . . . and with the scar across her
> stomach and a brace. And that, as they say, is it (Lentin,
> 1989, p. 216).

References

Adorno, Theodor (1949 [1973]). 'After Auschwitz' in Theodor Adorno, *Negative Dialectic*. New York: Continuum.

Ancel, Jean (1997). 'The Romanian campaign of mass murder in Transnistria, 1941–42' in R.L. Braham (ed.) *The Destruction of Romanian and Ukrainian Jews during the Antonescu Era*. New York: Columbia University Press.

Ancel, Jean (2000). 'Mas'ot haretsach hahamoni shel haromanim be-Transnistria: 1941-1942 (The mass murders in Transnistria 1941–1942)', *Bishevil Hazikaron (In the Path of Memory)*, Vol. 38, pp. 23-37.

Antisemitism World Report (1996). 'Romania'. London: Institute for Jewish Policy Research.

Appelfeld, Aharon (1999). *Sipur hayim (A story of a life)*. Jerusalem: Keter.

Arzi, Yitzhak (1999). *Davka Zioni (Glad to be a Zionist)*. Tel Aviv: Yedioth Aharonoth Books.

Bauman, Zygmunt (1989). *Modernity and the Holocaust*. Cambridge: Polity Press.

Bauman, Zygmunt (2000). 'The Holocaust's life as a ghost' in R. Fine and C. Turner (eds) *Social Theory after the Holocaust*. Liverpool: Liverpool University Press.

Benjamin, Lya (1997). 'Anti-Semitism as reflected in the records of the Council of Ministers, 1940–1944: An analytical overview' in R.L. Braham (ed.) *The Destruction of Romanian and Ukrainian Jews during the Antonescu Era*. New York: Columbia University Press.

Berenbaum, Michael (1997). 'Preface' in R.L. Braham (ed.) *The Destruction of Romanian and Ukrainian Jews during the Antonescu Era*. New York: Columbia University Press.

Braham, R.L. (1997). 'The exculpatory history of Romanian nationalists: The exploitation of the Holocaust for political ends' in R.L. Braham (ed.) *The Destruction of Romanian and Ukrainian Jews during the Antonescu Era*. New York: Columbia University Press.

Carp, Matatias (1946–48). *Cartea Negra (The Black Book)*. Bucharest: Atelierele Grafice Socec and Co.

Dawidowicz, Lucy (1975). *The War against the Jews 1933–45.* Harmondsworth: Penguin Books.

Delbo, Charlotte (1995). *Auschwitz and After.* New Haven and London: Yale University Press.

Eskenasy, Victor (1997). 'Historiographers against the Antonescu myth' in R.L. Braham (ed.) *The Destruction of Romanian and Ukrainian Jews during the Antonescu Era.* New York: Columbia University Press.

Fischer-Galati, Stephen (1993). *20th Century Romania.* New York: Columbia University Press.

Gallagher, Tom (1995). *Romania after Ceausescu: The Politics of Intolerance.* Edinburgh: Edinburgh University Press.

Gilbert, Martin (1993). *Atlas of the Holocaust.* Toronto: Lester Publishing.

Glassberg-Gold, Ruth (1999). *Etmolim Avudim: zikhronoteha shel nitzola (Ruth's Journey: A Survivor's Memoir).* Jerusalem: Yad Vashem.

Hirsch, Marianne (1997). *Family Frames: Photography, Narrative and Postmemory.* Cambridge: Harvard University Press.

Ioanid, Radu (1997). 'The fate of Romanian Jews in Nazi occupied Europe' in R.L. Braham (ed.) *The Destruction of Romanian and Ukrainian Jews during the Antonescu Era.* New York: Columbia University Press.

Ioanid, Radu (2000). *The Holocaust in Romania: The Destruction of Jews and Gypsies under the Antonescu Regime, 1940–1944.* Chicago: Ivan R Dee, in association with the US Holocaust Memorial Museum.

Lagerwey, Mary (1998). *Reading Auschwitz.* Walnut Creek: Alta Mira Press.

Langer, Lawrence (1991). *Holocaust Testimonies: The Ruins of Memory.* New Haven: Yale University Press.

Lavi, T. (ed.) (1969). 'Pinkas hakehilot' in *Encyclopaedia of Jewish Communities, Romania, Vol. 1.* Jerusalem.

Lentin, Ronit (1989). *Night Train to Mother.* Dublin: Attic Press.

Lentin, Ronit (2000). *Israel and the Daughters of the Shoah: Re-occupying the Territories of Silence.* Oxford and New York: Berghahn Books.

Lentin, Ronit (2001). 'Memory and forgetting: Gendered constructions of silence in the relationship between Israeli Zionism and the Shoah'. Occasional paper, Mediterranean Programme, Robert Schumann Centre, European University Institute, Firenze.

Litani, Dora (1981). *Transnistria.* Tel Aviv.

Ofer, Dalia (1999). 'Life in the Transnistria ghettos' in Ahron Weiss (ed.) *Yad Vashem Research Vol. 25.* Jerusalem: Yad Vashem.

Ofer, Dalia (2000). 'The Shoah in Transnistria: the murders and the Jewish response,' *Bishevil Hazikaron (In the Path of Memory),* Vol. 38, pp. 38–49.

Ofer, Dalia (2001) 'Children and youth during the Holocaust' in Shmuel Almog, David Bankier, Daniel Blatman and Dalia Ofer (eds.), *The Holocaust: History and Memory: Essays Presented in Honor of Israel Gutma*n. Jerusalem: Yad Vashem.

Palti, Sonia (1983). *El Me-ever LaDnierster: Na'ara Be'eretz Gzeira (Exile in TransDniester).* Tel Aviv: Moreshet/Sifriat Poalim/Hakibbutz Ha'artzi Hashomer Hatzair.

Ringelheim, Joan M. (1997). 'Genocide and gender: A split memory' in Ronit Lentin (ed.) *Gender and Catastrophe.* London: Zed Books.

Sand-Landau, Rita (1992). *Mei Hanahar Adamu . . . (Red ran the river...).* Tel Aviv: Reshafim.

Segev, Tom (1991). *Hamillion Hashevi'i: HaIsraelim vehaShoah (The Seventh Million: The Israelis and the Holocaust).* Jerusalem: Keter.

Shachan, Avigdor (1988). *Bakfor Halohet: Getaot Transnistria (Burning Ice: The Ghettos of Transnistria).* Tel Aviv: Bet Lochamei Hagetaot and Hakibbutz Hameuchad.

Shafir, Michael (1985). *Romania: Politics, Economics and Society, Political Stagnation and Simulated Change.* London: Frances Pinter.

Shafir, Michael (1997). 'Marshall Antonescu's postcommunist rehabilitation: *cui bono?*' in R.L. Braham (ed.) *The Destruction of Romanian and Ukrainian Jews during the Antonescu Era.* New York: Columbia University Press.

Simyonovics, Mark (1999). *Transnistria — the Hell*. Film for television, directed by Zoltan Terner and produced by Mark Simyonovics: Israel Educational Television.

Steigman-Carmelly, Felicia (1997). *Shattered! 50 years of Silence: History and Voices of the Tragedy in Romania and Transnistria*. Scarborough, Ontario: Abbeyfield Publishers.

Tec, Nechama (1986). *When Light Pierced the Darkness*. Oxford: Oxford University Press.

Volovici, Leon (1997). '*Leumiut, antishemiut veanchei ruach beRomania bishnot ha-30* (Nationalism, antisemitism and intellectuals in Romania in the 1930s)', *Bishevil Hazikaron (In the Path of Memory)*, Vol. 38, pp. 4–11.

Chapter 7

THE CONCEPT OF CHILDHOOD AND THE EXPERIENCE OF CHILDREN IN VIOLENTLY DIVIDED SOCIETIES

Marie Smyth

It is a great honour to contribute to the inaugural Heaney Lectures. It is a particular pleasure because I am a former student of Professor Heaney's, having studied English literature at The Queen's University of Belfast in the 1970s, during the darkest days of the Troubles. I have been invited to prepare a lecture on childhood, a subject that I have been examining in relation to the Troubles in Northern Ireland. In honour of Professor Heaney and what he taught me and many other students, I have decided to use literature alongside the drier and less poetic social sciences.

In the lecture, I wish to discuss the concept of childhood, and differentiate between the concept of a *child* and that of *childhood*. Then, I would like to consider the transformation that occurs in personal life in violently divided societies, and examine this transformation through the eyes of children in two violently divided societies, namely South Africa and Northern Ireland. I will examine some of the evidence of children's experience of the Troubles. I would then like to examine how, if at all, the concept of childhood is applicable in violently divided societies, and finish by posing a question, 'Who, then, experiences childhood?'

THE CONCEPTS OF 'CHILD' AND 'CHILDHOOD'

The distinction between the concept of a child and that of childhood is central to the argument advanced here. A child is a person under a certain age: for the purposes of international protocols such as the United Nations Convention on the Rights of the Child, a child is a person under the age of 18 years of age. Childhood, on the other hand, is, according to Ariès (1960), a social institution developed in the eighteenth century amongst the bourgeoisie, associated with the development of education and schooling as a moral instruction outside the home, and involving the social segregation of children from adult worlds. Earlier concepts of childhood applied only to children under the age of five, whilst those over five were not socially separate from adults and were often economically active.

Being chronologically young, therefore, has not always been associated with 'childhood' as it is currently understood. More recent educational theories, however, conceptualised children as innocent and in need of adult protection. By the end of the nineteenth century, the concern with the moral development of children, together with changing patterns of work and family life, led to new conceptualisations of the responsibility of parents, and the importance of privacy, morality and domesticity in the development of the child (Bowlby, 1953). The introduction of regulation of the workplace, with the Factory Acts in the 1840s, began a broader process of constructing the notion of citizenship, a concept that included children. Eventually, this was to lead to the legal enshrinement of children's rights to education and welfare. Implicit in this enshrinement of the rights of the child is the notion that the state has the right to intervene within the family to protect the child from parents or to ensure that the child has access to, for example, education. The conditionality of parental rights over children has been further institutionalised in the United Kingdom by the latest Children's Acts.

Childhood, then, is not a universal or timeless phenomenon. It is relatively recent in human history, a socially constructed phenomenon that acts as a 'deep structure', as Chomsky would have it, a 'generative grammar' regulating and reproducing not merely the language but the expectations and content of relationships between actual adults and actual children. In contemporary western society childhood is manifest by, for example, compulsory schooling; the legal protection of children from economic, sexual and other forms of exploitation; legal limits on the age of marriage and criminal responsibility; tolerance of the ignorance and mistakes of children; and the vesting of the 'duty to care' in all adults, not merely those who are parents. The concept of childhood implies adult recognition of the special needs and vulnerabilities of children and the attendant adult moral and legal duties towards children.

THE APPEARANCE AND DISAPPEARANCE OF CHILDHOOD

With the advent of increased divorce rates, the failure of absent fathers to make appropriate provision for their children, the increased involvement of women in work outside the home, the 'discovery' of childhood sexual abuse, and the rise of the single-parent family, the perception of the position of children in society is seen as more precarious. Some, such as Postman (1982), argue that childhood itself is disappearing in Western society. Others discuss various aspects of childhood, such as the globalisation of childhood (Boyden, 1990) and the various experiences of childhood, alongside the concept of childhood itself (James, 1993; Prout and James, 1990; Goldson, 1997; Scraton, 1997). Contradictions in contemporary conceptualisations of childhood are pointed up by, for example, public attitudes to the Jamie Bulger case in Britain. There, attitudes were challenged by the simultaneous presentation of children in contemporary culture as manifestly vulnerable, innocent and lacking in agency (Jamie Bulger) and conversely as feral, dangerous and wicked (his killers). It can be argued that

Bulger's killers were disqualified as 'children' in public opinion. Nonetheless, this reinforces the idea of childhood itself as essentially innocent and lacking in agency. Whatever the configuration, the Bulger case served to illustrate the continued existence of a concept of childhood. This was not always the case, however. Childhood did not always exist. Postman (1982) argues that, in Europe's descent into what is called the dark ages

> four points are often overlooked [that are] particularly relevant to the story of childhood. The first is that literacy disappears. The second is that education disappears. The third is that shame disappears. And the fourth, as a consequence of the other three, is that childhood disappears (Postman, 1982, p. 10).

Postman is positing three main societal conditions for the existence of childhood: literacy, education, and shame. Since our concern is with the impact of war on childhood, it is pertinent to examine the impact of war and civil conflict on these three factors in our two selected societies, namely Northern Ireland and South Africa.

Important differences between Northern Ireland and South Africa should be noted initially, since there are dangers in direct comparisons. Northern Ireland is located in the northern hemisphere, and enjoys many of the advantages of developed, first world education, albeit mediated by peripherality and conflict. South Africa, although arguably the most developed of the African nations, is a developing country, in which the level of access of a large section of the population to basic health care, housing, clean water and education is more characteristic of the developing world.

LITERACY AND EDUCATION

There have been changes to education provision in South Africa during the transition to majority rule. In 1996, some 19 per cent of the population in South Africa over 20 years old had no education, and about 24 per cent had some primary education only. Between 1979 and 1998, the number of candidates taking senior certificate examinations increased by 548 per cent and the number passing increased by 267 per cent. The proportion of degrees and diplomas awarded to whites decreased from 53 per cent in 1995 to 45 per cent in 1996 and the number awarded to Africans increased from 35 per cent in 1995 to 44 per cent a year later. Between 1991 and 1996, the total higher education awards increased by 154 per cent and decreased among whites by 3 per cent in the same period (Forgey et al., 1999).

In Northern Ireland, although there have been continuing instances where schools have been attacked, and where wearing a particular school uniform renders a child the target of sectarian violence, compulsory education has continued to be provided throughout the period of the Troubles. Patterns in the take-up of further and higher education have been shaped by the conflict, typified by the increased 'greening' of the student population in universities due to the tendency of Protestant students to opt to attend Scottish or English universities. Nonetheless, literacy is high — in comparison to South Africa and the developing world — and access to education is relatively good.

Despite this, inequalities related to the conflict, and the conflicts themselves have impacted on both literacy and access to education in both societies. Those who have suffered most as casualties in the conflict have also the least access to education and the highest rates of illiteracy. However, neither literacy nor education entirely disappeared. Thus these two conditions (education and literacy) which, according to Postman, are necessary for the existence of childhood still exist in both societies, even if access has been unevenly distributed.

SHAME

Explaining the disappearance of childhood in medieval society, Postman asserts:

> Immersed in an oral world, living in the same social sphere as adults, unrestrained by segregating institutions, the medieval child would have had access to almost all of the

forms of behavior common to the culture. The seven-year-old male was a man in every respect except for his capacity to make love and war. . . . The coarse village festival depicted by Breughel, showing men and women besotted with drink, groping for each other with unbridled lust, have children eating and drinking with the adults. . . . Breughel's paintings . . . show us two things at once: the inability or unwillingness of the culture to hide anything from children, which is one part of the idea of shame, and the absence of what became known in the sixteenth century as *civilité*, which is the other part. There did not exist a rich content of formal behavior for youth to learn.

According to Postman's analysis, shame, then, historically has depended on two factors: *civilité*, and the concealment of certain things from children. Before we can examine these, however, it is necessary to consider the manner in which war and violent societal division affect personal life, since it is within the sphere of personal and family life mainly that childhood is or is not formed and maintained.

WHAT HAPPENS TO PERSONAL LIFE IN VIOLENTLY DIVIDED SOCIETIES?

Under conditions of national emergency and political upheaval, individuals experience a sense of personal danger and threat to life. Yet such threats are not personal to the individual. Rather, they are directed at a group. In the case of South Africa, the group is racially defined; in the case of Northern Ireland the group is defined by affiliation to a national identity. Under such conditions, social and spatial polarisation occurs, serving the urgent need to differentiate between enemies and friends. Group identification can be — and has been in too many cases — a matter of life and death. Such extreme circumstances invariably lead to an accentuation of the group identity, at the expense of individualisation. The dominant discourse about the conflict, as expressed in the public domain, is characterised by expressions of anger and grievance.

Fear, grief, loss and despair are often relegated to (the isolation of) the private domain, except when such loss can be used politically by being represented as evidence of the barbarism of the enemy.

These processes inexorably lead to a kind of transformation of personal life in violently divided societies. Observers note a form of stoicism, a humour, a shying away from certain issues and topics. This phenomenon was powerfully and poetically described by Arundhati Roy in her book, *The God of Small Things,* in the context of Indian political upheaval. The male character, Larry McCaslin (an outsider), describes his wife, Rahel (an insider), as follows:

> But when they made love he was offended by her eyes. They behaved as though they belonged to someone else. Someone watching. Looking out of the window. At a boat in the river. Or a passerby in the mist in a hat. He was exasperated because he didn't know what that look meant. He put it somewhere between indifference and despair. He didn't know that in some place, like the country that Rahel came from, various kinds of despair competed for primacy. And that personal despair could never be desperate enough. That something happened when personal turmoil dropped by at the wayside shrine of the vast, violent, circling, driving, ridiculous, insane, unfeasible, public turmoil of a nation. That Big God howled like a hot wind, and demanded obeisance. That Small God (cozy and contained, private and limited) came away cauterised, laughing numbly at his own temerity. Inured by the confirmation of his own inconsequence, he became resilient and truly indifferent. Nothing mattered much. Nothing much mattered. And the less it mattered, the less it mattered. It was never important enough. Because Worse Things happened. In the country that she came from, poised forever between the terror of war and the horror of peace, Worse Things kept happening. So Small God laughed a hollow laugh, and skipped away cheerfully. Like a rich boy in shorts. He whistled, kicked stones. The source of his brittle elation was the relative smallness of his misfortune. He climbed into people's eyes and became an exasperating expression. What Larry

> McCaslin saw in Rahel's eyes was not despair at all, but a
> sort of enforced optimism (Roy, 1997, p. 20).

Roy describes a world in which 'public and private concerns must compete for primacy' yet where personal concerns can *never* be important enough to claim this primacy. As a result the personal is *cauterised* — to assert the primacy of the personal is laughable. This inconsequence of the personal leads to resilience and indifference: '*Nothing mattered much. Nothing much mattered.*' A spiral of indifference is established: 'Poised between the terror of war and the horror of peace, Worse Things kept happening'. Peace is not to be trusted, one dare not hope. One must be prepared for war. Yet 'it is not despair, but a sort of enforced optimism' — a kind of stoicism — resting on a foundation of denial and silence.

SECRETS AND *CIVILITÉ*

What, then, of Postman's *civilité* and secrets? Since denial is all-pervasive, secrets are the rule rather than the exception. Nothing is discussed. There is no language with which to discuss. More importantly, there is no motivation to discuss, because *'nothing mattered much. Nothing much mattered'*. Within such an ambience, the life experiences of children often expose them to death, destruction, brutality and corruption. But *'nothing mattered much. Nothing much mattered'*. Children's experience is often surrounded by denial and silence, which can function as a kind of open secrecy, and inarticulacy, a failure to name. Secrets are articulated once, in order to become known as secret. These phenomena are seldom articulated.

Children often see things that, by the 'normal' rules of childhood, should not be seen by children, and know things that should not be known. In war and violent conflict, in spite of international conventions and protocols, *civilité* is, more often than not, the first casualty. Children experience brutality, injury, death and threat at first hand, either as victims, witnesses or indeed as perpetrators. An overview of the deaths of children, and selected reports made by children of their experience of the Troubles in Northern Ireland illustrate this.

Deaths of Children and Young People in the Troubles

Analysis of those killed in the conflict since 1969 illustrates the particular vulnerability of children and young people. An age breakdown of deaths in the Troubles reveals that of all age groupings examined, the 18–23 age group contains the highest number of deaths — 898. This age group alone accounts for 25 per cent of all deaths in the Troubles. People of 29 years and under account for over half the deaths in the Troubles to date. The numbers killed in each age group up to the age of 24 reveals that both the 15–19 and the 20–24 age groups have a death rate that is higher than that for the total population. If age groups are examined in more detail, it can be seen how the death rate rises from around age 12 onwards, peaking around 19 or 20. Clearly adolescence is a high-risk period, and only in early adulthood does the death risk begin to diminish. The risk remains relatively high for young adults, and one only sees substantial diminution after the age of 40. The risk for those in their late teens and early 20s is unmatched by any other age group. If we see death as a surrogate for the effect of the Troubles as a whole, we can surmise that similar patterns will occur amongst the population of those injured. High levels of participation by young people in rioting and other street activities ensures that in relation to injury, young people are also the highest risk group.

Gender

As in the overall population, the risk of death in the Troubles for young males is much greater than for young females. Out of a total of 273 children killed, 209 (76.5 per cent) were male. Surveys of both adults (Fay et al., 1999) and children (Smyth and Scott, 2000) reveal that males have more direct experience of violence, both as victims and perpetrators, and consequently are more at risk of death and injury. In both genders, the death rate is related to age.

The highest number of deaths is at the age of 19 and 20, with declining death rates for all age groups thereafter. Twenty-year-old
males constitute 13.48 per cent of all males under-24 killed, whilst
19-year-old females constitute 15 per cent of all females under-24
killed. Deaths of people aged 24 and under account for 35.46 per
cent of all deaths in the Troubles, whilst people of 24 and under
account for roughly 40 per cent of the total population. The data
on age demonstrate how Northern Ireland's Troubles have been a
killer of young people, particularly young men. Again, one can
see the death rate steadily rise as age increases from birth onwards, and rise substantially at around the age of 12 to 14 years
old. Gender is clearly a factor in the social context, particularly in
relation to the culture of violence.

Geographical Distribution

An examination of the distribution of death of those under the age
of 25 and those under the age of 18 by the location of the home of
the victim reveals that the deaths of children are concentrated in a
relatively small area of Northern Ireland.* The six Northern Ireland postal areas BT11–15 (North and West Belfast) and BT48
(Derry/Londonderry city) account for 33.5 per cent of all deaths
under the age of 25 and an astounding 58 per cent of all deaths
under the age of 18. Clearly, death in the Troubles affected some
children more than others — namely young males, resident in
North and West Belfast, Derry or the border regions.

A positive correlation can be shown between the areas where
the risk of death was greatest and the highest levels of deprivation
and family poverty. Children live not only with poverty, but also
with the effects of militarisation, and the interplay between vio-

---

* Since British soldiers could serve in Northern Ireland in the early 1970s from
the age of 16, some of those under 18 who died were British soldiers possessing
home addresses in Great Britain. The age for serving in Northern Ireland was
raised subsequently to 18. Still, a substantial number of the 353 people killed in
England, Scotland and Wales under the age of 25 were members of the British
Army.

lence and deprivation. The implications for Northern Ireland's children are that some children in the worst-affected areas are likely to have a great deal of experience of the violence of the Troubles, whilst others have very little. This has major ramifications for our understanding of the situation of children in Northern Ireland. Because of the localisation of conflict, research that takes a representative sample of young people in Northern Ireland will tend to over-estimate the experiences of children in low violence areas like Bangor, whilst underestimating the experience of children in high violence areas such as North or West Belfast. To speak of the 'average Northern Irish child's' experience is misleading, since children's experience is widely diverse, with a substantial proportion of children having little experience of the Troubles, and a relatively small number of children having very intense, concentrated and prolonged experiences of life-threatening Troubles-related events.

Those Responsible for the Deaths

The analysis of the deaths of those under-18 years according to perpetrator must take suicide into account, where there is an indication that suicide can be attributed to the Troubles. Similarly, fatal road accidents where the Troubles were a causative factor are included. This method of accounting yields figures higher than the official figures, which exclude these deaths. The analysis presented here also includes a number of people who died from crossfire, where it has not been possible to attribute the death to any one perpetrator, and children killed by Army vehicles. The same pattern emerges in both the under-25 and the under-18 age groups (Table 7.1).

Republican paramilitaries, in particular the IRA, are responsible for the largest number of deaths of those under 18, followed by Loyalist paramilitaries, then the security forces, particularly the British Army. A substantial share (25 per cent) of all Catholic deaths is due to Republican paramilitaries. Republican paramilitaries are also responsible for the largest percentage of deaths in the under-18 age group (33 per cent) and in the total population (56 per cent). However, whilst Republican paramilitaries are responsible for 56 per cent of all deaths, and 55 per cent of those under the age of 25, they are responsible for a much smaller share (33 per cent) of deaths under the age of 18. Loyalist paramilitaries are responsible for 27.4 per cent of all deaths, compared to 21.3 per cent of deaths under the age of 25 and 28 per cent of deaths under the age of 18. Security forces are responsible for 10.7 per cent of all deaths, 17.5 per cent of deaths under the age of 25, and 25 per cent of deaths under the age of 18. Although Republican paramilitaries bear responsibility for most deaths in all age categories, there is a marked increase in the share of total deaths of young people due to the security forces' activities — particularly with regard to those under the age of 18.

Table 7.1: Responsibility for Deaths of Under-18s

	Number	Per cent
Republican paramilitaries	89	33
Loyalist paramilitaries	77	28
Security forces	68	25
Accidental shootings	10	4
Other/don't know	15	5
LVF	1	—
Real IRA	13	5
Total	273	100

Cause of Death

The largest share of deaths of children has been caused by shooting and this is true of deaths caused by both paramilitary organisations and security forces (Table 7.2).

A substantial number of children were killed in explosions that are most likely the responsibility of the IRA. Whilst the British Army have concentrated their efforts in combating the IRA and other paramilitary organisations, making their focus of attack the communities which house paramilitaries, the IRA has also dealt with the threat of informers and performed a controversial role in policing communities in which they are based. The fact that the IRA have killed more people in the under-25 compared with the under-18 age group may reflect these factors.

Table 7.2: Cause of Death of Under-18s

Cause	Number	Per cent
Shooting	139	51
Explosions	100	37
Burns	9	3
Assault	7	2.5
Accident	7	2.5
Rubber Bullets	7	2.5
Army vehicle	4	1
Total	273	99.5

The security forces' employment of armoured vehicles accounts for a small but significant number of children's deaths. In such circumstances, the driver's vision is restricted, and vehicles that are under attack from stones and other missiles, and which are therefore moving fast in restricted spaces, can constitute a particular hazard to children. There are no reliable figures for the numbers of children and young people who have been killed and injured in this manner, but the cases that are verifiable are included here. A number of deaths due to rubber and plastic bullets are also tabulated.

Plastic Bullets

Policing in Northern Ireland has necessitated the development of strategies to combat street violence and rioting. Successive security strategies have deployed CS gas, water cannon and, most consistently, rubber and plastic bullets. Rubber bullets, which were used initially, were replaced by plastic bullets in response to complaints about the severity of the injuries they caused. Table 7.3 further analyses these deaths, which have particular relevance to children and young people.

Table 7.3: Deaths from Plastic Bullets by Age and Gender of Victim

Age at Death	Male	Female	Total
10	1	0	1
11	2	0	2
12	0	1	1
13	1	0	1
14	0	1	1
15	2	0	2
16	1	0	1
18	1	0	1
21	2	0	2
22	1	0	1
33	0	1	1
40	1	0	1
41	1	0	1
45	1	0	1
Total	14	3	17

Since these bullets, also referred to as baton rounds, are used in riot situations against unarmed combatants, they are frequently deployed in situations involving young people and children. The purpose of such weapons is to disable people temporarily, and thereby allowing the security forces to control the situation. By 1991, the use of plastic bullets in Northern Ireland had led to the deaths of an estimated 17 people, ten of whom were aged 18 or under. RUC officers fired four of the fatal bullets, and members of the British Army fired the remainder. Numbers of others have been injured, some very seriously and permanently, by plastic and rubber bullets. Arguably, children are more vulnerable because of the size of the bullet relative to the size of a child's body. There has been a campaign to ban the use of plastic bullets in crowd control and riot situations because of the danger to children. To date they remain in use, albeit in a modified form.

Religious Affiliation of Children and Young People Killed

Table 7.4 shows the number of under-18s killed, according to the religious community they have been identified with.

Table 7.4: Politico-Religious Affiliation of Those Killed under Age of 18

Affiliation	Number	Per cent
Catholics	199	72.5
Protestants	53	19
Non-Northern Ireland*	16	6
Unknown	5	2
Total	273	99.5

*Non-Northern Ireland refers to those who are not residents of Northern Ireland.

Catholics constitute the largest group, and whilst this reflects the distribution of all deaths between the two communities, the differential is much more stark in the case of young people. While Catholics comprise just over 43 per cent of all deaths and 48 per cent of those under-25 killed, they provide almost 74 per cent of those killed under the age of 18. While total Catholic deaths outnumber Protestant deaths both in relative and absolute terms, the overall scale of the difference is much less than it is for the under-18 age group.

Political Affiliation

Table 7.5 details the political and social affiliation of those killed. Just over 45 (45.6) per cent of those killed under the age of 25, and 80 per cent of those killed under 18 were civilians. Security forces constitute 34.2 per cent of those killed under-25, but only 1.95 per cent of those under-18 killed were members of the security forces. Republican paramilitaries composed 15.7 per cent of those killed under the age of 25, and 15 per cent of those killed under 18. Finally, 3.3 per cent of those under-25 killed, and 2 per cent of those killed under-18, were loyalist paramilitaries.

Table 7.5: Status of Those Killed under the Age of 18

Status	Number	Per cent
Civilians	218	80
Republican paramilitaries	40	15
Loyalist paramilitaries	7	2
Security forces	5	2
Unknown	3	1
Total	273	100

Clearly, most children and young people killed in the Troubles were civilians, and this is particularly true of the under-18 age group. Children and young people have, however, also been combatants (see Figure 7.1).

If we are to judge by the death figures, the grouping within whose ranks children and young people are most likely to die as combatants is the Republican paramilitaries — the IRA (21 deaths) and their junior wing, Na Fianna (14 deaths) have contributed the majority, with the Official IRA providing 3 combatants under-18 killed, and 2 from the Fianna branch of their organisation. Both other categories of combatants — Loyalist paramilitaries (UDA with 4 deaths and UVF with 3) and the security forces (British Army with 5 deaths, 3 of whom died in England) — have also recruited and armed persons legally defined as children.

Figure 7.1: Deaths of Combatants under 18, 1969–97

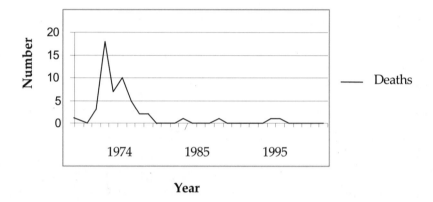

Deaths of combatants under 18 peaked in 1972, when there were 18 casualties (see Figure 7.1). The subsequent decline in the number of combatants under 18 who died is partly related to the fact that the British Army no longer sends soldiers under 18 to serve in Northern Ireland — although they continue to recruit from this age group.

Punishment Shootings and Beatings

The lack of an acceptable police force, largely in Nationalist areas, and the need to control 'anti-social behaviour' within the community has led to both Loyalist and Republican paramilitaries exercising a form of rough justice in their respective communities. The Good Friday Agreement and the early release of prisoners led to the increased involvement of political activists and former prisoners in a range of community activities. Parallel with this, members of local communities have demonstrated an increased readiness to take their complaints about the plague of vandalism and local crime to paramilitary 'authorities' in their community in the expectation that 'something will be done'. Within communities, tolerance for violence is high, and a belief in corporal punishment and physical punishment as a deterrent is widely shared. As is apparent from Figure 7.2, violent methods of punishing offenders are used. More recently, attempts to find non-violent methods — community restorative justice — of dealing with anti-social behaviour have been initiated, largely in Nationalist areas.

Figure 7.2: Paramilitary Assaults, 1998–2000, All Ages and Under 20

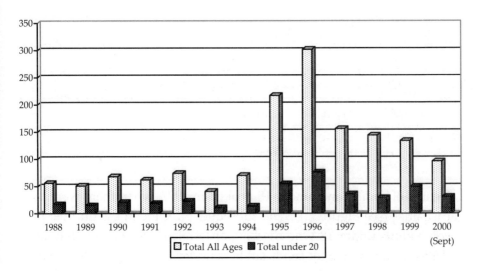

Nonetheless, violent methods are still in use. Table 7.6 presents a breakdown by Loyalist and Republican of reported punishment beatings from 1988 onwards. It is apparent from this that both Loyalist and Republican beatings follow the same pattern, peaking in 1996. Some differences emerge after 1996, with an overall decline in the total numbers of Republican beatings, whereas the Loyalist beatings increased in 1998 and 1999. The overall decline in the number of beatings masks an increase in the number of under-20 year olds beaten in 1999.

Table 7.6: Casualties of Paramilitary Violence: Assaults

Year	Loyalist All Ages	Loyalist under 20	Republican All Ages	Republican under 20	Total All Ages	Total under 20
1988	21	8	35	9	56	17
1989	23	5	28	10	51	15
1990	21	2	47	19	68	21
1991	22	6	40	13	62	19
1992	36	8	38	15	74	23
1993	35	9	6	2	41	11
1994	38	7	32	7	70	14
1995	76	16	141	39	217	55
1996	130	25	172	51	302	76
1997	78	18	78	18	156	36
1998	89	15	55	14	144	29
1999	90	30	44	19	134	49
Jan-Sept 2000	56	18	40	13	96	31

Since punishment beatings do not involve the use of firearms, they are less likely to be regarded as breaches of paramilitary ceasefires. However, incidents of punishment shootings (Table 7.7 and Figure 7.3), as well as being more damaging to the victims, are arguably more hazardous for the political process and so have caused various politicians publicly to question the status of various organisations' ceasefires. Thus, there was a virtual cessation of punishment shootings in the period following the 1994 ceasefires. Subsequently, however, both Loyalist and Republican groups reverted to using them, with Loyalists responsible for a total of 216 shootings between 1995 and September 2000, which is substantially greater than the Republican figure of 129. Of these, 30 Republican shootings and 39 Loyalist shootings were of people under 20.

Table 7.7: Casualties of Paramilitary Violence: Shootings

Year	Loyalists All Ages	Loyalists under 20	Republicans All Ages	Republicans under 20	Total All Ages	Total under 20
1988	34	5	32	14	66	19
1989	65	12	96	32	161	44
1990	60	13	46	18	106	31
1991	40	8	36	10	76	18
1992	72	11	61	20	133	31
1993	60	13	25	7	85	20
1994	68	13	54	15	122	28
1995	3	—	—	—	3	—
1996	21	6	3		24	6
1997	46	10	26	7	72	17
1998	34	3	38	9	72	12
1999	47	12	26	6	73	18
Jan-Sept 2000	65	8	36	8	101	16

Some of the Loyalist shootings and beatings may well be related to the Loyalist feuds that proliferated sporadically during that period. Concern has been expressed politically that the continued use of violent methods by paramilitaries associated with some of the political parties involved in the Assembly indicates a less than total commitment to non-violence. Politicians, councillors and MLAs have an interest in solving problems in local Catholic communities, such as anti-social behaviour and law and order issues. Yet problems of anti-social behaviour continue to dog the communities they represent, and some of their electorate consider violence a legitimate and effective method of solving such problems. As a result, Sinn Féin representatives report that they come under pressure from their constituents to promote and pursue violent methods of dealing with these issues.

Figure 7.3: Paramilitary Shootings, 1988–2000

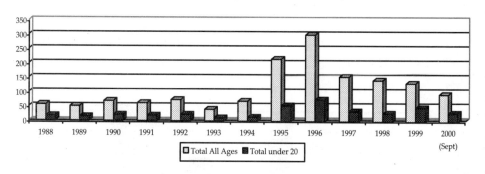

Nor are deaths and injuries the only ways in which the Troubles in Northern Ireland have affected children and young people. A recent survey (Smyth and Scott, 2000) of young people in Northern Ireland has revealed that young people's lives are constrained in a variety of ways as a result of the ongoing conflict. Figure 7.4 shows the response to a question that asked whether respondents (aged 14–16) had ever had to hide their religion. Half said that they had had to do so, with Catholics featuring disproportionately.

Figure 7.4: 'Have Had to Try to Hide My Religion'

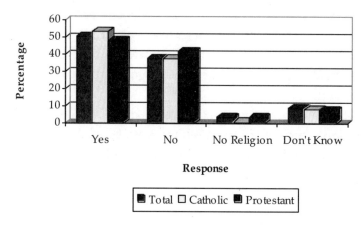

Figure 7.5 shows that about 13 per cent of respondents reported 'a lot' of experience of being threatened or verbally abused, with over half the respondents having some experience of such behav-

iour. Again, Catholic respondents reported more such experiences than Protestants.

Figure 7.5: Incidence among Young People of Being Threatened or Verbally Abused

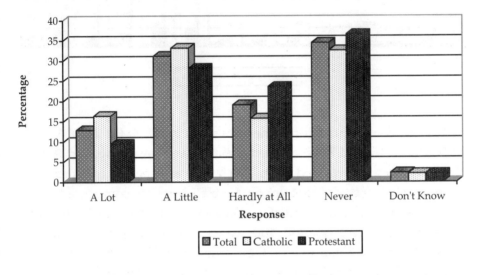

Figure 7.6 represents the response to a question about being bullied because of religion. Less than 10 per cent reported a lot of experience of sectarian bullying, with Catholics having somewhat more experience than Protestants. However, 31 per cent of Protestants and 29 per cent of Catholics reported a little experience of sectarian bullying, and 39 per cent of young people had no experience of it.

Figure 7.7 shows the response to a question about avoiding certain places because of the likelihood of abuse. About half of all young people said that they avoided certain places for this reason.

Figure 7.6: 'Do Students at Your School Get Bullied Coming to or Leaving School because of Their Religion?'

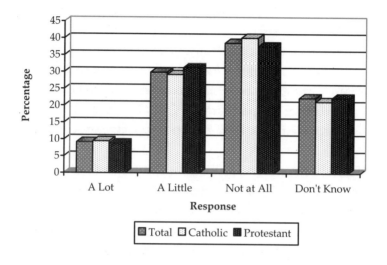

Figure 7.7: 'Do You Avoid Particular Places because of the Risk of Being Verbally Abused or Threatened?'

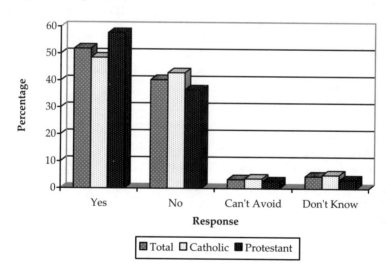

Children and young people in Northern Ireland grow up in a society where residential segregation accordingly to religion is intensifying, and where children are largely educated at separate schools — Protestants at the state schools and Catholics in Catholic-maintained schools. As a result, for some children and young people contact with the 'other' community can be very limited. Respondents to the survey were asked about cross-community contact; 77 per cent of Protestants and 66 per cent of Catholics reported that they had some cross-community contact, but 7 per cent of both Catholics and Protestants do not have contact on principle. A further 24 per cent of Catholics and 12 per cent of Protestants reported that they had no opportunity to have such contact.

Young respondents were also asked about their experiences of the Troubles. Tables 7.8 to 7.11 show their responses, with Table 7.8 showing some of the less severe experiences, and Table 7.11 showing very severe experiences. From Table 7.8, it emerges that a majority of young respondents have experience of straying into the 'wrong' area, and feeling they have to watch what they say.

Table 7.8: Common Experiences

	Very often %	Occasionally %	Seldom %	Never %	Don't Know%
Straying into an area where I didn't feel safe	13.5	31.5	29.5	21.5	4.2
Getting stopped and searched by security forces	9.2	14.5	18.9	53.5	3.9
Feeling unable to say what I think or being wary in the presence of other people because of safety issues	16.8	30.4	23.1	21.7	8.1
My parents having to take extra safety precautions to secure my home or workplace	7.9	12.9	15.9	55.6	7.8
Having to change my normal routes, routines or habits because of safety	8.1	14.7	16.7	54.6	6.2

Table 7.9 shows responses to questions about more direct experiences, such as ending friendships because of the sectarian divide, having schooling disrupted, and experiences of military organisations acting as punishment agencies. A substantial minority of respondents reported getting into physical fights as a result of the Troubles, and significant numbers reported having their schooling disrupted.

Table 7.9: Young People's Experiences of the Troubles

Event/Experience	Very Often %	Occasionally %	Seldom %	Never %	Don't Know %
Having to end friendships or having relationships disrupted because of the sectarian divides	4.0	7.4	9.4	74.7	4.5
Getting into physical fights about the troubles	8.1	14.2	16.0	58.7	3.0
Having my schooling disrupted by the troubles	3.1	9.9	18.7	62.2	6.1
Had experiences of military organisations acting as punishment agencies	4.6	8.0	11.2	61.4	14.8

Table 7.10 examines respondents' severe experiences of the Troubles. Some 12.5 per cent of respondents reported having their home attacked, and over 11 per cent report having to leave their homes temporarily because of the Troubles; a further 3.5 per cent report having to leave their homes permanently, and over 4 per cent report having their homes destroyed as a result of the Troubles. Clearly, for a small but significant number of children and young people, the Troubles has been a major disruption to their lives.

Table 7.10: Young People's Severe Experiences of the Troubles

Events/Experiences	Very Often %	Occasionally %	Seldom %	Never %	Don't Know %
Having my home attacked	2.4	3.2	6.9	85.8	1.6
Having to leave my home temporarily	1.0	3.9	6.5	87.1	1.4
Having to leave my home permanently	1.2	0.7	1.6	94.9	1.6
Having my home destroyed	0.9	0.5	2.7	94.1	1.7

Table 7.11 examines other severe experiences. Over half (52.5 per cent) of young people admit to being caught up in a riot, and almost 17 per cent claim to have witnessed a shooting. A further 14 per cent report having seen people killed or seriously injured. Some 12 per cent report having a member of their immediate family killed.

Table 7.11: Other Severe Experiences of the Troubles

Event /Experience	Several Times %	More than Once %	Once %	Never %	Don't Know %
Being caught up in a riot	16.1	16.8	19.6	45.2	2.3
Witnessing a shooting	3.3	4.0	9.6	81.3	1.9
Having a work colleague attacked	2.6	6.7	8.2	79.4	3.1
Having a work colleague killed	1.2	1.4	3.4	91.5	2.5
Having a neighbour attacked	3.5	8.1	17.1	68.0	3.3
Seeing people killed or seriously injured	1.9	4.0	8.5	83.0	2.6

Event /Experience	Several Times %	More than Once %	Once %	Never %	Don't Know %
Having a close friend killed	4.8	10.8	16.5	65.9	2.0
Being injured in a bomb explosion	0.8	0.7	3.6	93.1	1.8
Being injured in a shooting	1.1	1.1	4.1	91.7	2.0
Having a member of my immediate family injured	4.1	6.7	14.4	71.7	3.1
Having a member of my immediate family killed	1.6	2.9	7.5	85.1	2.9
Having another relative injured	3.9	8.9	16.4	65.8	5.0
Having another relative killed	2.0	3.5	8.5	80.0	6.0

In Table 7.12, over 16 per cent of respondents reported having their education affected by the Troubles, and over 20 per cent report disruption to their family life and relationships due to the Troubles.

Table 7.12: Have the Troubles Ever Affected

	Yes %	No %	Don't know %
Your schooling, education or training?	16.6	78.2	5.2
Your home life, family relationships?	22.6	72.7	4.7
Your social life, hobbies and leisure?	42.3	54.0	3.7
Your other activities, such as shopping?	37.8	58.0	4.2

From Table 7.13, it is apparent that just over 4 per cent of young people reported that the Troubles had 'completely ruined their lives', and over 14 per cent said that the Troubles had 'severely altered the path that their lives would have taken'.

Table 7.13: Effects of Troubles on Young People

Do you think the Troubles have:	Yes %	No %	Don't know %
Completely ruined my life	4.2	91.3	4.4
Damaged my health	4.4	92.1	3.4
Caused me to lose loved ones through deaths	12.4	82.9	4.6
Physically damaged me/or my family	15.5	79.4	5.2
Severely altered the path my life would have taken	14.3	78.0	7.6
Led to me or my family leaving our home through intimidation or attack	10.5	84.3	5.2
Influenced where I have chosen to live	32.0	62.5	5.4
Made members of my family emigrate	21.7	71.9	6.4
Made members of my family and/or me seriously consider emigration	22.7	71.6	6.0
Divided members of my family against one another	9.6	85.3	5.2
Made me fearful for my own and my family's safety	29.8	63.2	7.0

Over 20 per cent reported that the Troubles had led members of their family to emigrate, and just under 10 per cent said that the Troubles had divided their family. Table 7.14 shows that 5 per cent of all respondents, and just under 7 per cent of Catholic respondents and 2.5 per cent of Protestants, felt that the Troubles had completely changed their lives. Conversely, over 10 per cent overall and 16 per cent of Catholics and 23 per cent of Protestants felt that the Troubles had not affected them at all.

Table 7.14: Effect of Troubles on Young People

How much has your experience of the Troubles affected you?	Overall %	Catholic %	Protestant %	Male %	Female %
Completely changed my life	5.0	6.9	2.5	7.5	2.9
Radically changed my life	4.0	5.1	3.2	4.9	3.3
Made some changes to my life	30.6	32.5	29.0	30.8	30.8
Made a small impact	34.6	34.8	34.8	31.7	37.0
Not at all	10.6	16.1	23.8	19.5	19.4
Don't know	6.0	4.7	6.8	5.6	6.6

CIVILITÉ IN VIOLENTLY DIVIDED SOCIETIES

The reported experience of two children, one from Northern Ireland one from South Africa, further illustrate the *timbre* of children's experience. First, the words of Jolene McAllister, from Belfast:

> Well, I am fifteen now, and I was with my aunt whenever [i.e. when] she was killed in Flax Street. We'd just walked around the corner and there was a whole lot of shots fired and my aunt was shot. There was a fella beside her and he was shot too. . . . When they shot my aunt, I was linking arms with her . . . I wouldn't go out. I was too scared. . . . Then, I was going to school, but I had to walk past the place where she was killed to get to school. That stopped me from going to school. . . . I walk past it now, so I do, but I wouldn't walk past it then. . . . I lost a brother seven months ago. He was my best brother. He was dead close to

me, that one. He was killed. The INLA shot him in Turf Lodge seven months ago. Then his girl[friend] had his wee child two weeks after he was killed. That wrecked me, so it did. It wrecked our whole family because he was the special one out of the whole family. I don't know what it was . . . it's not as if he was stupid or anything, but he would do stupid things. . . . My Mummy's changed. I get out of school on a half day on Friday, and there'd be times that my Daddy wouldn't be in and the child [her dead brother's child] would be over. And she'd lift the child up to the photo and all and say, 'There's my son, there's your Dad!' you know, and talk to the photo. . . . At night she does not sleep. You'd be lying in bed, and you'd hear her crying, then she puts out her fag and then she lights another one. All she does is smoke. . . . Will I tell you what happened to my cousin? My friend and me, a wee girl that stays with me at the weekend, walked in the door and she went into the living room. And I went in and says to Mummy, 'Is the dinner ready?' She said, 'It's nearly ready now.' And I went back into the living room, and I'd heard our cousin's voice. . . . I said, 'There's our cousin! Come on out and we'll get a laugh.' And she said, 'Well, I'm watching television . . .' And I went out, and we were all standing there talking. My Mummy said to me, 'Did you shut the front door?' and I said 'No!' She said, 'Go and shut it!' I said, 'Hold on! I'll shut it in a minute!' Our child had fallen — my wee brother. He'd fell, and my cousin lifted him up and put him on his shoulders, and went to walk out the back to my Daddy and my cousin's brother. This fella came in [the front door] and he shouted, 'Yo!' And we turned round, and he'd shot my cousin in the neck. My wee brother fell off [my cousin's shoulders] and hit his head off a gas barrel, and my wee brother was just lying there. My cousin went down on his two knees and he got back up again. He went to run for your man, but he slipped in his own blood. And the man said to him, 'Die, you Fenian bastard!' And he shot him another twice in the head — another two times in the head — and just walked out. I just stood there and looked at him. I froze — I couldn't do nothing. And my mother was on the ground. She'd collapsed. She didn't know what was happening. And then she got up and she run. My Daddy run in and then run out again, and I was still standing there. Then I walked out and seen my Mummy. She'd collapsed over my cousin's car. And I walked in to the kitchen, and my wee brother was lying over my cousin, all full of blood. My wee brother was only two. I just didn't want to talk to anybody. . . . And then going up to the graveyard made you think back. 'Why didn't I shut our front door, and all, when I was told to? Like my Daddy, my cousin and my brother, if they had of all been in the kitchen, I'm sure they would have been dead too. There was nothing they could have done because your man had a gun. I was never out of Mass. Now, I wouldn't even go to Mass. . . . That's been from my aunt was killed. I haven't been to Mass from my aunt was killed. . . . I think when I say my prayers at night, that's my Mass over and done with. I don't ask God for anything (Smyth and Fay, 2000, pp. 111–18).

Jolene did not ask God for anything because God was powerless to give her any of the things she wanted. She wanted her brother back; she wanted her aunt back; she wanted her cousin back. The 'small God' of family relations and ties of affection was powerless in the face of the God of war, and she knew this. She watched her mother run, whilst she walked. She, Jolene, had seen it all before. She went to her two-year-old brother covered in blood, whilst her mother collapsed.

There is little evidence of *civilité* in her account of the world she lives in; awful deeds and sights are not shielded from Jolene's child eyes. There are no secrets. She even knows the name of the gunman who shot her cousin, who has never been prosecuted for this act. This gunman, and the one who shot her aunt, do not hold their fire until the children are safely out of harm's way; nor do the other adults attend to the children, shield or protect them.

They are disabled by their own various states — battle fury, collapse and shock.

Jolene's account is mirrored by Sello Duiker's semi-autobiographical account of his life as a street child in Cape Town, South Africa. He lives on his wits on the streets of Cape Town, climbing Table Mountain to escape a drug dealer. He returns to Cape Town when he thinks it is safe:

> I watch the candle burn and think about the mountain and the cave. I wonder who's staying there now. Maybe that stupid man with the long hair will come back. And he'll say, Where's the boy who's full of shit? But I'm not a boy. I know I'm thirteen but I'm not a boy. On the streets boys my age support families. They give their mother money so that they can buy drugs and feed them nothing. They break into cars and steal small change from dashboards to that they can buy needles to inject themselves with poison. They mug old ladies and buy buttons. And when they are fucked out of their faces they cry about it till snot drips like water.
>
> A boy, I'm not a boy. I've seen a woman being raped by policemen at night near the station. I've seen a white man let a boy Bafana's age get into his car. I've seen a couple drive over a street child and they still kept going. I've seen a woman give birth in Sea Point at the beach and throw it into the sea. A boy? Fuck off. They must leave me alone. I have seen enough rubbish to fill the sea. I have been fucked by enough bastards and they've come on me with enough come to fill the swimming pool at Sea Point (Duiker, 1999, p. 142).

Duiker, as a thirteen-year-old child, sees things that many adults have not seen — human depravity in all its aspects. Adults, far from being protective, are dependent, exploitative and oppressive. There are no secrets. Nothing is kept from this street-wise child. His portrayal of the brutality of his life as a child is a representation of the antithesis of *civilité*. Therefore, Duiker refuses childhood as a valid conceptualisation of his life experience.

Jolene, similarly, knows death, destruction and the limitations of adults, including God.

DOES CHILDHOOD EXIST IN VIOLENTLY DIVIDED SOCIETIES?

The concept of *childhood* is resisted by Duiker as a category that fits his experiential frame of reference. This resistance has a surface validity, and no doubt a similar position would be taken by Jolene and by other children with similar experiences, living in divided societies. However, neither Duiker's nor Jolene's experiences are universal or representative. Other children, by virtue of their geographical, racial, ethno-political or socio-economic location within that society, are not exposed to the same extent as Duiker or Jolene. Exposure to violence in any war-torn or divided society is differentiated by socio-economic position, geography and other factors. The difficulty of ensuring the protection of children from witnessing atrocities, or of shielding children from physical danger is related to the degree of threat and the proximity to danger and violence. Poor families, for example, are generally more at risk of exposure and experience more severe effects. Those families with multiple or protracted exposure to violence are almost invariably poor, and therefore vulnerable in other ways.

The primary agent for the care of children affected by violent conflict is the parent and the family group. Whilst some adults remain able to recognise the need to protect children, that recognition seems to be reduced by exposure to threat and danger. Adults exposed to traumatic and dangerous circumstances, often on an ongoing basis, may find it increasingly difficult to cope with the effects on them of their own exposure. In such circumstances, the capacities of adults to observe the needs of others may be compromised. Ultimately, in such circumstances, adults may not be able to ensure their own safety, let alone that of children. Furthermore, it is precisely those adults with the greatest amount of exposure (usually family members) who as a consequence are likely to experience the worst effects of violence. These are the adults who are most likely to be the caretakers of the children with the most exposure. Conversely, those adults with the least difficulty (and least cumulative exposure) are least likely to be *in situ* to implement the protection of children. These latter adults — observers from a relatively safe distance — may judge the former adults' failure to protect children in moral terms, without an understanding of their circumstances.

The accounts presented here describe situations that obtain in Northern Ireland and South Africa. Children *are* involved in prostitution, rape, drugs, killing and hatred. That children are so involved is shocking to us because we have a contemporary idea about childhood that relies on ideas of innocence, vulnerability and so on. We are shocked because we are removed from the situation, and are employing a judgement based on a distance from violence. Proximity and exposure to violence alters that judgement, reduces that shock. Children's involvement is less shocking when you, yourself, are close and exposed to violence. And even if it is shocking, proximity to violence — the experience of a gunman coming into your kitchen and shooting a family member dead — may render adults powerless, and victimised. The 'lived experience' of being in that kitchen with Jolene's mother can make the international protocols for the protection of children in places where there is armed conflict seem irrelevant. Very often it is the gunman, the perpetrators, the armed groups that have the power to take account of children. Yet, it is hard to think of an example when they have done so. However, the blame and moral approbation for the failure to provide attention and care to children such as Jolene or Sello Duiker is often directed at those with the least capacity to make such provision — their families — who are often themselves victimised and disempowered.

VICTIMHOOD

Within violently divided societies, cultures of victimhood develop. Victimhood is universally experienced and claimed by 'both sides'. In Northern Ireland particularly, paramilitary ex-prisoners, for example, lay claim to victimhood. Victimhood is characterised by the experience of suffering, loss and bereavement, powerlessness, helplessness, dependence, absolution from responsibility, expressed need for and moral entitlement to help. Victimhood is also used as a legitimisation of further violence, which is ultimately blamed on the original perpetrator. Thus responsibility for acts of violence can be removed from those who perpetrate them, *rendering them shame-free*. The culture of victimhood, where 'everyone is a victim', therefore is a factor in the erosion of shame in a society. Victimhood itself is thus a *kind of childhood*, widely experienced and reported in violently divided societies. This diminished facility for shame and lack of agency ultimately contributes to the lack of capacity to protect, take responsibility, and ensure the well-being of children and, thereby, to create and to sustain childhood itself.

CHILDREN AS AGENTS IN THEIR OWN LIVES

Yet the identities of children in violently divided societies are constructed by societal division, and children are not merely potential or actual victims. They are political and sometimes military agents. Violence and sectarian division has become a 'normal' and routinised part of contemporary childhood in Northern Ireland. Children's school uniforms mark them as one side or the other; they learn to keep to their own territory, and if they fail to do so it is 'their own fault' if they get attacked. Childhood is the time when citizens in Northern Ireland and in other divided societies acquire their absolutist identification with one or other side of the conflict. Indeed, that very absolutist identification demonstrates how thinking in violently divided societies tends to a form of bifurcated childish 'black and white' thinking that eschews complexity. Violence seems to push us inexorably to such bifurcation. Complexity is seen as a luxury indulged in by those who are safe. Children socialised into this stark world-view develop opinions and exercise political agency, as other children do. Children think and act politically. One of the many differences between South

Africa and Northern Ireland is the degree to which the political
and military contribution of children is recognised formally. In
South Africa, recognition of the role of students and school-based
activism involving street demonstrations and the deaths of many
children were among the forces that informed the development of
provision for children in the new constitution. In Northern Ireland, on the other hand, where children have continued to be ac-
tively involved in street violence, and recruited to membership of
armed groups, there is a lack of formal recognition of children's
role. This is at once a hopeful and a depressing augury — hopeful
in that perhaps it signals some residual shame at children's involvement, depressing in that it may rather be a sign of the general low status of children in the wider society.

WHO, THEN, EXPERIENCES CHILDHOOD?

According to Millay (1934):

> Childhood is not from birth to a certain age, and at a certain age
> The child is grown and puts away childish things
> Childhood is the kingdom where nobody dies
> Nobody that matters, that is.

If this is so, for children exposed to the terrors and losses of violent societal division, and for many adults who grew up with such
division and loss, childhood has never existed. The ability of
adults to protect children depends on the establishment of adulthood as a social, moral and intellectual state differentiated from
the state of childhood. Material conditions, such as militarisation
and continuing violence, can infantilise adults, and render them
powerless to fulfil these roles and functions. The recovery or introduction of a more graduated and nuanced understanding of
the situation of children depends on adults operating as adults,
thinking like adults, with the power and agency of adults.

Given the longevity of the conflict in Northern Ireland, in
South Africa and elsewhere, this will necessitate some people becoming adults without ever having had a childhood. The search

for ways in which this can be achieved is amongst the most important challenges in building peace. If we observe the lessons of history or, in psychological terms, the patterns of intergenerational transmission of grievance, then:

> In the ancient shadows and twilights
> Where childhood had strayed
> The world's great sorrows were born
> And its heroes made.
> In the lost boyhood of Judas
> Christ was betrayed (Germinal, *Vale and Other Poems*, 1931).

Amongst those who have never known childhood are some — perhaps only a few — possessed of the kind of dangerous power that is ignorant of its own might, that has never learned limits, or understood the consequences of its actions. Left to their/our own devices, it is they/we who will threaten the possibility of childhood for the current and future generations of children. If we are to achieve the state where, as Seamus Heaney puts it, 'hope and history rhyme' (Heaney, 1990) then finding ways of compensating for lost childhoods, in order to prevent further such losses, is imperative. The task is daunting. It is the task of helping those souls — ourselves — who have lost their childhoods forever to find a way through the foreign territory of peace, without falling back on the familiarity of war. It is hard to think of work that is more important.

References

Ariès, P. (1960). *Centuries of Childhood*. Harmondsworth: Penguin.

Bowlby, J. (1953). *Child Care and the Growth of Love*. Harmondsworth: Penguin.

Boyden, J. (1990). 'Childhood and policy makers: A comparative perspective on the globalization of childhood' in James, A. and Prout, A. (eds.) *Constructing and Deconstructing Childhood*. London: Falmer Press.

Duiker, K. Sello (1999). *Thirteen Cents*. Cape Town: Ink/David Philip.

Fay, M.T., Morrissey, M., Smyth, M. and Wong, T. (1999). *Report on the Northern Ireland Survey: The Experience and Impact of the Troubles.* Derry/Londonderry, INCORE / the United Nations University and the University of Ulster.

Forgey, H., Jeffrey, A., Sidiropoulos, E., Smith, C., Corrigan, T., Mophuthing, T., Helman, A., Redpath, J., and Dimant, T. (1999). *South Africa Survey 1999/2000: Millennium Edition.* Johannesburg: South African Institute of Race Relations.

Goldson, B. (1997). 'Childhood: An introduction to historical and theoretical analyses' in Scraton, P. (ed.) *Childhood in Crisis?* London: University College London Press.

Heaney, S. (1990). *The Cure at Troy: After Philoctetes by Sophocles.* Derry: Field Day.

James, A. (1993). *Childhood Identities: Self and Social Relationships in the Experience of the Child.* Edinburgh: Edinburgh University Press.

Millay, Edna St Vincent (1934). *Wine from Grapes.* New York: Harper and Bros.

Pattison, S. (2000). *Shame: Theory, Therapy and Theology.* Cambridge: Cambridge University Press.

Postman, N. (1982). *The Disappearance of Childhood.* New York: Vintage.

Prout, A. (ed.) (2000). *The Body, Childhood and Society.* Basingstoke: Macmillan.

Prout, A. and James, A. (1990). 'A new paradigm for the sociology of childhood? Provenance, promise and problems' in James, A. and Prout, A. (eds,) *Constructing and Reconstructing Childhood.* Basingstoke: Falmer Press.

Roy, A. (1997). *The God of Small Things.* New York: Harper Collins.

Scraton, P. (1997). 'Whose Childhood? What Crisis?' in Scraton, P. (ed.) *Childhood in Crisis?* London: University College London Press.

Smyth, M. and Fay, M.T. (eds) (2000). *Personal Accounts from Northern Ireland's Troubles: Public Conflict, Private Loss.* London: Pluto.

Smyth, M. and Scott, M. (2000). *The YouthQuest 2000 Survey: Young People's Experiences and Views of Life in Northern Ireland.* Derry/Londonderry: INCORE / the United Nations University and the University of Ulster.

Smyth, M. (1998). *Half the Battle: Understanding the Impact of the Troubles on Children and Young People*. Derry/Londonderry: INCORE/United Nations University/University of Ulster.

Chapter 8

EDUCATION AND HAPPINESS

Nel Noddings

Speaking in March 2000, William Bennett, former Secretary of Education in the United States, expressed concern that parents might be turning against the standardised testing movement. He observed:

> A recent survey showed that when parents are choosing a school for their child, high test scores are one of the *least* important factors in their decision. The most important: the child's happiness. Armed with public opinion, we can wear down the unions. But if parents go soft, we are done (quoted in Bracey, 2000, p. 139).

To want happiness for their children is, according to Bennett, to "go soft". He is a bit late in discovering that most parents want, first and foremost, happiness for their children. Probably he, too, wants his children to be happy, but apparently he would not make happiness the first criterion in choosing their school. Or perhaps his conception of happiness differs from that of the parents surveyed. Or, again, perhaps he is one of those who believe that a certain amount of misery is justified, even necessary, for future happiness. In any case, it is odd that happiness — some-

thing that figures so prominently in human hopes and dreams —
is so little discussed in education.

I would like to make a start at opening that discussion by exploring, all too briefly, a few basic questions: What is happiness?
Where might we find it; that is, in what domains of activity might
we seek it? How might schooling contribute to its achievement?

WHAT IS HAPPINESS?

Philosophers have found it useful to make a distinction between
happiness itself (if it can be defined) and those things that contribute to it. Aristotle (1985), for example, noted that we are likely
to identify happiness with health when we are unwell, with
wealth when we are broke, and so on. But these "contributors"
are not happiness itself. (Actually Aristotle wrote of *"eudaimonia"*
perhaps better translated as "human flourishing" than "happiness", but many writers simply refer to "happiness", and I will
follow that practice here.) A little later, when I ask about the
sources of happiness, I will not be looking for such contributors
but, rather, for the domains or spheres of activity in which they
are likely to be found. A basic question for Aristotle (one that he
answered ambiguously) was whether to regard happiness as a
comprehensive state (in which case we have to identify its com-
ponents) or something dominant and special in itself (Dunne,
1997; Rorty, 1980). The first position complicates philosophical
analysis, but the second has created problems for both educational and democratic thought.

What Aristotle suggested, in his second position, is sometimes
called the "intellectualist" view on happiness. It holds that theo-
retic or contemplative thought is superior to practical wisdom and
activity in the world. On the one hand, there is something lovely
about this; it supposedly points to the divine in human beings —
a capacity that lifts us beyond everyday affairs and concerns. On
the other hand, it creates a hierarchy of human activity that de-
values the practical and those who do the practical work of the

world. John Dewey (1916, 1929) pointed out more than once the pernicious effects of sharply separating theory and practice.

At the level of kindergarten to twelfth-grade schooling, we still suffer the effects of Aristotle's separation and hierarchical evaluation. In the US, for example, vocational education has been offered as an alternative to the traditional academic curriculum for more than 100 years (Kliebard, 1999). But it has almost always been treated as second-rate — a form of schooling for those who are "not up to" real education. Even Dewey argued against vocational education as it was designed early in the twentieth century because it seemed to foreclose opportunities instead of opening them up. Today, the trend is away from all forms of tracking on the grounds that "all children can learn" and all should experience the academic curriculum once reserved for a few. And this is recommended in the name of democracy and equality. The recommendation avoids the crucial question of whether this curriculum was ever the "best" for anyone and in what sense. Even if it is best for some, there is little reason to suppose it is best for everyone.

If we reject the Aristotelian hierarchy, we might take a very different approach. We might accord respect and dignity to all honest human activity. We might construct and provide rich and rigorous curricula to match a full range of human capacities and interests. To insist that all students will now be equal but, at the same time all will be cast in the Aristotelian "best" mode, is both unrealistic and undemocratic. That legacy persists in our present evaluation of physics and chemistry as better than mechanics, of mathematics as somehow superior to food science, of traditional literature as more acceptable than studio art or music.

The elevation of intellectual life over all other forms of human activity also colours perspectives on happiness. If it is thought that adult life can only flourish when the mind is highly trained in traditional ways, then parents are likely to insist that their children develop the forms of competence accorded the highest levels of respect. From such a perspective it may seem justifiable — even obligatory — to inflict the familiar forms of misery on school children. "Some day you will thank me for this", parents have insisted in every generation. Misery today for happiness tomorrow. Religious traditions, too, have contributed to this way of thinking.

But before we give way on this, let us consider a number of alternatives. A different view of happiness equates it with pleasure, and utilitarians have had to defend this conception in establishing their utilitarian principle. In describing the Greatest Happiness Principle, John Stuart Mill wrote: "by happiness is intended pleasure, and the absence of pain" (Mill, 1993, p. 144). However, if we follow Mill, we do not escape Aristotle's emphasis on the intellect, for Mill carefully describes the pleasures that are characteristic of a well-developed intellect and contrasts these sharply with those of a pig or a fool. Thus, once again we are urged to consider that which *should* give us pleasure because we are beings with a certain intellectual capacity. Indeed, Mill insisted that those who actually experience such pleasures would not give them up for mere sensual pleasures. This has a ring of truth for those of us in academe. However, we must acknowledge that we may be deceiving ourselves. Perhaps others experience pleasures far greater than our dry (or enormously exciting) intellectual ones. We can try to avoid the extremes (as Mill did in some passages) by insisting that all normally endowed human beings can be brought to experience at least some pleasures associated with intellectual activity but, of course, this claim could be made for almost any human activity, and now we have to say what we mean by "intellectual". It should not surprise us if we wind up with a hierarchy of intellectual pleasures. In any case, we are still elevating intellectual life over all other forms.

Recognizing all these complications, social scientists today often use Subjective Well-Being (SWB) as an operational definition of happiness (Lane, 2000). Armed with this definition, they can ask people questions ranging from "how much fun are you having?" to "does the future seem hopeful?" (Lane, 2000, p. 16). Answers to questions of this sort can then be correlated with answers to the straightforward question: taken all together, how would you say things are these days — would you say that you are very happy, pretty happy, or not too happy (Lane, 2000, p. 20)? Now, of course, we can spot difficulties with this approach right off. Doesn't one's mood matter? That can be addressed by repeating the questions at various intervals or by taking large samples so that we can drop the predictable percentage of people in a bad mood. Can we use this approach with children? Do people (not only children) really know what makes them happy? This is a deeper, very difficult question.

To complicate matters further, Robert Lane notes that, in western societies, "income, education, health, and intelligence (!) have all increased since World War II, but they have not made us happier" (Lane, 2000, p. 45). It is true that an increase in wealth that lifts people out of poverty makes them happier and, clearly, relief of pain and chronic illness increases happiness, but — beyond poverty — increased wealth does not often bring increased happiness, and lots of physically healthy people are unhappy. Well, what does bring happiness? Here we should be careful about settling on just one contributor, but Lane provides empirical evidence for companionship as the main source of happiness. If he is right, what does this mean for education? I will return to this question.

Perhaps we are on the wrong track entirely in identifying happiness with SWB. We all know people who, like Mill's fool or pig, seem perfectly happy living in a way that we deplore. How can the sloppy, beer-guzzling couch potato be happy? Aristotle and Mill would be aghast at the thought. Yet Mill, at least, would be equally aghast at telling adult persons what should make them happy, and this illustrates a paradox for liberal democracies. The emphasis on choice in such societies means that we do not interfere in the lives of adults unless they are harming others. Yet we cannot bring ourselves to have genuine respect for the ways of life that proliferate under a system of choice.

There seems, then, to be a normative aspect to definitions of happiness. SWB cannot be the whole story because, among other complications, a society just does not approve of many forms of pleasure-seeking that some people might choose. Moreover, societal disapproval affects an individual's SWB. I cannot feel "very happy" if I feel the disapproval of those around me and, of course, societal pressures work for both good and ill. They press people into behaviours and attitudes that may, in the long run, produce greater happiness; for example, as educators, we believe that good character has something to do with happiness, and so we continually try to find effective methods of character education. But social pressures also cause both temporary and permanent unhappiness by inducing envy, guilt, self-denial, self-indulgence, greed and a host of other ills. As a result of internal and external conflicts, many people are not sure what would make them happy or why they are unhappy. And not a few, nagged by an over-zealous conscience, religion or family, come to believe that they have no "right" to happiness.

Still another complication is that we can be happy in one part (domain) of our lives and unhappy in another. One may be happy in working life and unhappy in family life. To have a substantial effect on overall happiness, the domains assessed must be considered important in one's life. For example, John might be somewhat unhappy with his athletic performance but not regard the domain of athletics as important in his life. He can shrug off his lack of physical prowess and, while he recognises it, the deficiency does not affect his overall happiness. However, consider the effects that enormous family pressure might have on John. If, in John's intimate circle, rewards go to those who are athletically competent (and he is labelled a klutz), John may experience increased unhappiness.

Although we are not going to find a completely satisfactory definition of happiness in this small space and we will continue to stumble upon new features as we move along, it seems clear that there are objective and subjective aspects of happiness. Certain objective features — wealth, health, status — contribute to happiness, but they do not guarantee it. Much depends on how an individual feels, and we cannot overlook the possibility that happiness can sometimes be traced to personality. There may be such a thing as a "happy personality" (James, 1929). In all cases, happiness involves the satisfaction of needs and wants from those parts or domains of life thought (by the individual) to be important.

Now we can ask about the domains in which these satisfactions are likely to arise (or to cause unhappiness if they do not) and what education might do to promote them.

DOMAINS OF HAPPINESS

Before discussing domains in which happiness may be found or lost, I should say just a little about happiness with respect to stages of life. In this series, we are particularly interested in childhood and, certainly, childhood has figured prominently in accounts of happiness. Childhood is often identified, too romantically I think, as a period of innocent and undiluted happiness. Poetry has encouraged this view. But even those who think it is a mistake to romanticise childhood feel that there is something especially poignant and morally suspect about an unhappy childhood. We want childhood to be happy, but we do not want to secure that happiness at the expense of future happiness. This too we must keep in mind for later discussion. Here I will concentrate on the domains of activity in which we seek happiness.

The first task is to choose a set of categories that do not prejudice the analysis at the outset. I want to avoid one that separates the intellectual and manual, cognitive and non-cognitive, spiritual and mundane, and so on. How are our ordinary lives organised? Most of us recognise a separation (at least in hours) between paid work and personal life, so let us name these as two important categories. A third domain might be labelled "civic" or "community" life. In a child's life, these three domains might be labeled "home", "school", and "street" or "play yard". We know from a multitude of studies that children experience these domains as sharply separate. As we think about happiness and education, we need to ask where children find happiness in present experience and also how best to prepare them for future happiness.

Notice right at the start that public schools in liberal democracies pay very little attention to preparation for personal life. Most of our attention goes to preparation for higher forms of education, and thus for the world of paid work. We do give some lip-service to preparation for civic life, but most of our attention in this area goes to national histories, voting rights, and the like. It is preparation for civic life writ large, not for, say, neighbourhood life. Civic life, as interpreted in school, is not a domain in which many of us seek happiness. The domain of community comparable to the child's street or play yard is absorbed almost entirely into the category of personal life. For most of us this is the domain of greatest possibility, anyway, so let us start there.

Consider one major task faced by every adult — that of making a home. The historian Theodore Zeldin remarks:

> If it [making a home] is one of the great personal and collective works of art that all human beings spend their lives attempting to raise up and to keep from falling down, then the art of creating homes, as distinct from building houses, still has a long way to go, and still remains within the province of magic. Instinct or imitation are not enough to make a home (Zeldin, 1994, p. 393).

One reason that the making of homes is still dependent on "instinct or imitation" is that we simply do not take preparation for that great art seriously. It was for a time taken seriously, but for women only. If women were educated at all in the eighteenth and nineteenth centuries, they were educated to be homemakers. But, of course, this form of education was considered intellectually inferior to that offered men. To count as important, any course or programme of education had to prepare one for the public world, not the private world. This legacy exerts its influence today. Courses (few and far between) in homemaking or child-rearing are rarely accepted for college entrance credits, and they are widely regarded as courses for those who do not quite measure up academically.

But I am not advocating a semester of sewing and another of cooking. I am asking a deep philosophical question: what does it take to make a home? And I am asking it in connection with the question of happiness. If the domain of personal life — in particular, home life — is one of the great arenas in which happiness may be found, why do we not give it more attention in schools? One reason, already suggested, is that homemaking has been considered "women's sphere", one requiring no special preparation — just the apprenticeship of daughters to mothers. Today, when daughters rightly expect to claim a place in the public world, they need (or, at least, will be required to undergo) an education exactly like that of their brothers. Then, it would seem, if homemaking is to grow beyond instinct and imitation, both sons and daughters may need special preparation for this great art, since they will be expected to share in its practice.

Another reason — a complex one — for its neglect is the very division under discussion and how it has been interpreted in liberal democratic theory. Adults in a liberal democracy are to be free to pursue their private life in any way they choose, provided their choices do not preclude similar choices by others. The fierce protection of privacy in home and family life is part of this legacy of separation. Schools are to concern themselves with preparation for public life; homes (and religious institutions, if a head of family chooses to belong) should control and direct preparation for private life. Of course, this was hypocritical right from the start, because all-female schools did prepare girls for home life, though in a manner that did not threaten the privacy and autonomy treasured by male heads of households.

However, once we are convinced that the topic is one of the first importance for human flourishing, we can begin to explore its intellectual depths. Then the enterprise loses its innocence. It might well threaten the status and organisation of the entire school curriculum. Here I confess to being of two minds. On the one hand, I want to argue that questions of homemaking are profoundly philosophical and worthy of rigorous intellectual study. On the other, I would hate to see the topic subjected to the tedious and pompous rigmarole characteristic of academic life. I do not think schools kill curiosity and creativity in everything they do, but it is a near thing. Guarding against that result is a topic for another lecture, but I will touch on it toward the end of this one. Let us suppose for now that homemaking could be well taught if we chose to do so.

Gaston Bachelard provides an intriguing start for the phe- nomenological study of home and homemaking. He writes of the house:

> [F]or our house is our corner of the world. As has often been said, it is our first universe, a real cosmos in every sense of the word (Bachelard, 1964, p. 4).

As Bachelard analyses the house, it becomes clear that he is talk- ing about a home and not just a shelter from the elements. He says:

> If I were asked to name the chief benefit of the house, I should say: the house shelters daydreaming, the house protects the dreamer, the house allows one to dream in peace. Thought and experience are not the only things that sanction human values. The values that belong to daydreaming mark humanity in its depths. . . . It derives direct pleasure in its own being (Bachelard, 1964, p. 6).

Thus a home shelters not just the body, but the imagination. One's first home is "physically inscribed in us", writes Bachelard. "It is a group of organic habits" (Bachelard, 1964, p. 14). It is coloured by reality, imagination, longing, actual and created memories. Litera- ture, art and song are filled with descriptions of it and longing for it.

And what metaphors it has invited! Bachelard discusses doors, windows, corners, creaking stairs, cellars, attics, chests, drawers, polished tables, nests, and locks in all their real and metaphorical meanings. He invites us to think about our own "Blue Beard" rooms and our fear of cellars. He speaks of reading a house or room, and this wording leads us to other, like, ideas. John Elder (1998), for example, talks of "reading the mountains of home" and of "hiking a poem". Edward Casey (1993) asks us to think of rooms (and houses) as extensions of our bodies. We are reminded in all these readings of just how important *place* is in our lives. Think for a moment about how we might "read a room". How is it read by a detective? By an artist? By a child? By a dog? By a burglar? By a vampire?

From the utterly practical, through daydreaming, arises the image, and the image (unanalysed, warns Bachelard) begets a new being: "this new being is happy man" (Bachelard, 1964, p. xxix). He does not mean that one has to be a poet to be happy, nor that poets are always happy; often they are not. But there is something in the image that contributes immeasurably to human flourishing, and it does not stand in need of scholarship. "It is the property of a naïve consciousness", writes Bachelard; "in its expression, it is youthful language" (Bachelard, 1964, p. xix). All the more reason to treat what is close to home with both reverence and wonder. And here we have uncovered something that adds to our conception of happiness. It is neither raw pleasure nor philosophical contemplation; it is something with roots in the earth and branches in the heavens.

When we read the poems of Hardy, Frost, Rilke, Whitman or Heaney, we find them filled with ordinary things — apples, calves, wild roses, gates, fodder, a spoon-bait, beggars, polished linoleum; everyday activities — peeling potatoes, mending wall, playing ball, hiking a trail; and ordinary jobs — clerking, fishing, farming, laying bricks, draining pastures, driving trucks, selling hardware, teaching children and so on. Who could despise his own work when he sees it celebrated by Walt Whitman? But here is another preview of what must be considered in educating. While we give all children opportunities to learn so that they can be happy in Aristotle's image (or yours and mine?), we should take care not to cause them to think less of the lives their parents have led and of those many of them will also lead. As Whitman put it, we must say to children: "Why what have you thought of yourself?/Is it you then that thought less of yourself?" (Whitman, 1982, "A Song for Occupations", p. 90).

Beyond the house and its everyday objects and activities is a region, and again we find it odd that the love of place so celebrated in art and so often a factor in both child and adult happiness is neglected in schools. In the United States, our emphasis is on educating for a global economy; it is an education proudly (and stupidly) designed to transcend place. I visited a classroom recently in which a teacher told visiting parents, "this is a biology class; in here we study living things". Except for the captive human beings, there was not a living thing (visible) in that room. There wasn't even a picture of a living thing! One would never know from its appearance or its subject matter that this school sits within walking distance of the Atlantic Ocean and not far from a fascinating natural region called the Pine Barrens — an area so interesting that the essayist John McPhee (1968) addressed a whole book to it. Today's schools ignore it, but place figures prominently in the happiness of individuals, and it is also central to creative work. The poet W.B. Yeats said, "Creative work must have a fatherland".

The house and what lies beyond it are clearly places in which happiness is often found. But a home contains people and, if today's social scientists are right, companionship is the single greatest factor in producing the subjective sense of well-being. How well do we prepare children for companionship? If we can believe the figures given to us by Lane and other social scientists, the answer has to be "not very well", since years of education do not correlate highly with happiness and, thus, presumably not with the satisfactions gained through companionship.

In today's school, we insist that all children study algebra and geometry but, in fact, relatively few will use what they learn there in later life. Indeed, some years ago the comedian Fran Leibowitz urged high school students "to remain unconscious in algebra class. I assure you", she said, "in real life, there is no such thing as algebra". Of course, she exaggerated somewhat. Algebra and other forms of mathematics are enormously important for some purposes and for some people. But the majority could get by well with knowledge of only a few topics in academic mathematics. In contrast, all of us face the tasks of making a home and finding companionship, and most of us become parents. When these great tasks are treated at all in school, they are "add-ons", designed to address a social emergency such as teenage pregnancy, and they never achieve the status of respectability granted to the traditional disciplines.

When we think of preparation for personal life, we think also of development of the *person* who will find (or fail to find) happiness in personal life. Consideration of the person suggests some attention to the spiritual, ethical and personality features of life. Schools usually do something in the line of moral education, but often character education (the approach most often used today) concentrates on socialisation and control. Current programmes in the US, for example, emphasise the inculcation of traditional moral virtues, but they often neglect the kind of social virtues identified by David Hume (1983). Hume reminded us of "a manner, a grace, an ease, a genteelness . . . which catches our affection" (Hume, 1983, p. 72), and he insisted that these qualities have something to do with ethics precisely because they contribute to human happiness.

Today's care theorists (Noddings, 1984, 2002) agree with Hume, and they give some moral credit to the second member — the cared-for — in caring relations. How good we can be depends at least in part on how others treat us. It is easier to parent a sunny, responsive child than a sullen, withdrawn one; easier to teach agreeable, eager students than resistant ones; easier to treat hopeful, cooperative patients than those who have given up and fail to follow directions.

A thoroughly relational view puts less emphasis on moral heroism and more on moral interdependence. Recognising the domain of human interaction as the principal arena of happiness, it concentrates on creating the conditions under which people are likely to interact with others in mutually supportive ways. Insofar as certain agreeable qualities contribute to these conditions, we value them: politeness, wit, cultivated taste, unhurried serenity, a talent for listening, hospitality. And we are led to re-define responsibility as response-ability, the ability to respond positively to others and not just to fulfil assigned duties. When we think seriously about happiness and education, we extend the range of qualities we seek to develop.

HOW MIGHT SCHOOLS CONTRIBUTE?

Most teachers, like parents, want their students to be happy, but they are pressed by their work and by the ethos of market democracies to think of happiness in terms of economic and academic success. When teachers accept the market definition of happiness, they often feel justified in using coercion, creating boredom (unintentional, but unavoidable), and inflicting misery — all in well-intentioned efforts to ensure happiness "some day". At the opposite extreme, some teachers would (if they were allowed) reject not only coercion but even persuasion and, following A.S. Neill (1960), justify their decision in terms of present happiness. Just let the kids be happy.

A better way is harder, more complex, and more exciting. In this better way, we have to balance today's happiness with that of the future. We cannot neglect the quality of present experience, but neither can we ignore what will follow. The best of all possible classroom experiences would create interest and joyful engagement now and contribute to satisfaction, contentment, or happiness in the future. In this last part of the paper, I want to suggest some concrete things teachers might think about. Clearly, in discussing such large topics, I can only give examples, but I hope they will point to some larger guiding principles.

One guiding principle with which we might start is this: every act of coercion raises a question. Must we do this? Is the coerced activity clearly in the best interest of the child? Might something more congenial to the child work as well or even better? If we must coerce, what help will we offer? At the root of such thinking is a strong belief that caring relations contribute to happiness, and so we want to maintain such relations. In many cases, we will decide that coercion is not really necessary. The topic we had in mind and that brought resistance can easily be replaced by another that encourages the same skills and matches the child's interests.

Among the topics that interest children and will continue to be important to them throughout their lives are friendship (and other relationships), health, hospitality, existential questions (does life have meaning?), recreation and a relationship to their dwelling places. There are many others, of course, but teachers would make a good start to consider these when planning. Let's look at just one of these (mentioned earlier) — love of place.

There is increasing evidence that children need a connection to nature (Kahn, 1999; Nabhan and Trimble, 1994); indeed, we may all be affected by biophilia (Wilson, 1984) — the need for that connection. In the decades since World War II, education in the US has drastically reduced attention to natural history and concentrated more on the principles and vocabulary of technical branches of science. Kids learn the parts of a plant, but not how to grow one. They rarely learn to identify the shrubs and trees indigenous to their own region. They learn the difference between plant and animal cells, but not how to protect and love the animals that are their pets. Recall the scene in Dickens' *Hard Times* in which the teacher Gradgrind rejects the description of a horse offered by a child who actually works with the animals and praises the highly technical definition parroted by a child who has nothing to do with horses: "Quadruped. Graminivorous. Forty teeth, namely twenty-four grinders, four eye-teeth, and twelve incisive . . .". Of what use is such a definition to the average child, and what does it contribute to possible happiness? Do children learn in school about the centuries-old relationship between humans and some animals? Do they learn that the companionship of animals is thought to extend and make happier the lives of lonely old people? Thousands upon thousands of pet animals are put to death every year in the Unites States after abandonment, sometimes after neglect and mistreatment. Yet our big worry in science education is to raise test scores. To love a place, to explore it, to understand the creatures that live there and the conditions necessary for their survival is part of a happy life. It has almost always figured prominently in accounts of happy childhood.

Appropriate attention to natural history is not only educative, it helps to connect the domains of human activity. It recognises the great childhood joy of exploring the outdoors and the deep adult satisfaction of making a home in a place one loves. Careful study of one's own immediate environment has been a starting place for serious study in the lives of many scientists, writers and artists. Moreover, it can lead quite naturally to ecological sensitivity and enhanced recreational opportunities. Best of all, however, it can connect school to another — better loved — part of a child's life, and child life to a lifetime of appreciation for the world around us.

Study of the natural world of their immediate environment can also be used to help children integrate their school studies. Consider this passage from Twain's *Huckleberry Finn*:

> It's lovely to live on a raft. We had the sky, up there, all speckled with stars, and we used to lay on our backs and look up at them, and discuss about whether they was made or just happened — Jim allowed they was made, but I allowed they happened; I judged it would have took too long to *make* so many. Jim said the moon could a *laid* them; well, that looked kind of reasonable, so I didn't say nothing against it because I've seen a frog lay most as many, so of course it could be done. We used to watch the stars that fell, too, and see them streak down. Jim allowed they'd got spoiled and was hove out of the nest (Twain, 1982, p. 742).

This passage could be well used in science, mathematics and social studies as well as English classes. It is a violation of the child's spirit and the adult's search for meaning to keep school subjects rigidly separated from each other and from life itself.

Educators should consider a host of topics that might affect a child's future personal life, but we have to consider the world of work, too. Today, in the United States at least, this is the focus of our attention. We want every child to succeed, and this has come to mean that every child should be prepared for college and the sort of work that requires a college education. What of all the children who will become bus and truck drivers, retail sales clerks, appliance repair people, construction workers, material handlers, heavy equipment operators, railway engineers and conductors, house painters, plumbers, bakers, farm workers, beauticians, postal workers, cooks, waiters, hotel clerks, house and office cleaners, auto mechanics and sales people, dog and horse groomers, telephone/electric line workers, prison guards, hospital attendants, grounds keepers, maintenance workers, managers of laundromats and dry cleaning shops, installers of burglar alarms, carpet layers, window washers, steel workers, fishermen, sailors, caterers, cashiers, chimney sweeps, roofers, makers of china and glassware, decorators, musicians, florists, entertainers, moving men . . .? And what would happen to our society if no one were willing to do this work? Do these people represent failures of schooling, or do we fail them when we lead them to believe that only economic success *is* success?

Perhaps every child should hear Walt Whitman's lovely "Song for Occupations" and be invited to create a new song for the present day in their own place. It is commendable, of course, to give every child an opportunity to choose college-related study if they are so inclined, but no child should be made to feel that other forms of work are only for those who are not "up" to the work that really counts. This is a delicate and difficult issue, but teachers who think it through carefully may begin to stretch the standard curriculum so that it includes the interests and talents of all children and not just the few.

Education, of all enterprises, cannot neglect what I earlier called the "normative" aspect of happiness. In the better of his two conceptions of human flourishing, Aristotle (like most thoughtful teachers before and after him) put great emphasis on that component of happiness that arises from the practice of virtue. According to this view, people cannot really be happy unless they have a sound character and exercise the virtues characteristic of such a character. If we take the view of those who use SWB as the definition of happiness, Aristotle's claim is doubtful. Yet most of us in education believe something like it. We hope that children will learn to derive some happiness from doing the right thing, from satisfying the demands of their souls. We shrink from people who are happily untroubled by the misery of those around them. Still, there is a kind of happiness that creeps through, even in the presence of pain and misery, when we know that we have done what we can to improve things. Thus education for happiness must include education for *un*happiness as well. Children should learn (something many seem to know almost instinctively) that sharing the unhappiness of others, paradoxically, brings with it a form of happiness. This is a major conclusion reached by care theorists who argue that those things we do to improve the relations of which we are part will work for our benefit as well as that of others.

Finally, I want to say something about the oft-vaunted pleasures of the mind that we as educators are supposed to promote. For me, they are real but, like Whitman, I do not despise what gives pleasure to others, nor do I insist that others must get pleasure from what pleases me. However, because I have always loved learning, reading, thinking, teaching, discussing, I would like children to have opportunities to share these pleasures. How can we provide such opportunities?

For example, should we introduce children to poetry in school? Poetry can help us to connect the various domains of life. It gives delight. It helps us to find a bit of happiness in unhappiness and a core of unhappiness in momentary happiness. It can contribute through the power of the image to happiness now and in the future. I have never encountered a child under, say, seven who does not love poetry. But I almost never encounter a teenager who likes it. What have we done in our schools? We have wrecked the experience of poetry. We have poisoned something that we say we teach because of the lifelong delight it offers. Whereas the best poetry connects us to everyday life, school-taught poetry separates us even farther from it. Do kids really have to know the difference between dactylic hexameter and iambic pentameter? (We might like them to hear the difference.) Do they have to take apart every phrase and metaphor? Do we have to give tests on poetry? When we say that we are offering something to children that should increase their lifelong happiness, we should take care not to destroy the possibility. Some things, even in schools, should be offered as gifts — no strings, no tests attached.

In my own mathematics teaching and in introducing graduate students to elementary logic, I have often used *Alice in Wonderland* for its wonderful examples of logic and illogic. But I do not give tests on it! It is a free gift, offered to increase pleasure and the possibility of incidental learning. G.K. Chesterton remarked on the proclivity of teachers to wreck that which should be shared with delight. He wrote:

> Poor, poor, little Alice! She has not only been caught and made to do lessons; she has been forced to inflict lessons on others. Alice is now not only a school girl but a school mistress. The holiday is over and Dodgson is again a don. There will be lots and lots of examination papers, with questions like: (1) What do you know about the following: mimsy, gimble, haddocks' eyes, treacle-wells, beautiful soup? (2) Record all the moves in the chess game in *Through the Looking Glass,* and give diagrams. (3) Outline the practical policy of the White Knight for dealing with the social problem of green whiskers. (4) Distinguish between Tweedledum and Tweedledee (quoted in Gardner, 1963).

Not everything can be learned incidentally, but many things can be. Much of value sticks to us, as Frost said, "like burrs" where we walk in the fields. There should be lots of free gifts in education, lots of aimless but delight-filled walks in the fields of learning. It does not hurt, either, to pause now and then and ask children and ourselves: how much fun are you having?

CONCLUSION

I certainly have not answered the question of what happiness is or where we might find it or how schools should promote it in anything like a complete way. I have suggested that happiness is a topic enormously rich and complex for educators to consider. Choosing a few promising topics, I have offered ways in which teachers might balance today's happiness (which should never be ignored) with the promise of tomorrow's happiness, and the happiness (or unhappiness) actually felt by children with the happiness (or unhappiness) they should feel. I have suggested, too, ways of connecting the major domains of life in which happiness is found and promoting qualities and conditions that enrich relations and thus contribute to happiness. This is, perhaps, good enough for a start.

References

Aristotle (1985). *Nicomachean Ethics* (trans. T. Irwin). Indianapolis: Hackett.

Bachelard, G. (1964). *The Poetics of Space* (trans. M. Jolas). New York: Orion Press.

Bracey, G. (2000). "The 19th Bracey report on the condition of public education", *Phi Delta Kappan* 82, no. 2, pp. 133-44.

Casey, E.S. (1993). *Getting Back into Place*. Bloomington: Indiana University Press.

Dewey, J. (1916). *Democracy and Education*. New York: Macmillan.

Dewey, J. (1929). *The Quest for Certainty*. New York: G.P. Putnam's Sons.

Dunne, J. (1997). *Back to the Rough Ground*. Notre Dame, Indiana: University of Notre Dame Press.

Elder, J. (1998). *Reading the Mountains of Home*. Cambridge: Harvard University Press.

Gardner, M. (1963). *The Annotated Alice*. New York: World.

Gilligan, J. (1992). *Violence*. New York: G.P. Putnam's Sons.

Hume, D. (1983). *An Enquiry Concerning the Principles of Morals*. Indianapolis: Hackett.

James, W. (1929). *The Varieties of Religious Experience*. New York: Modern Library.

Kahn, P. (1999). *The Human Relationship with Nature.* Cambridge: MIT Press.

Kliebard, H. (1999*). Schooled to Work: Vocationalism and the American Curriculum 1876–1946.* New York: Teachers College Press.

Lane, R.E. (2000). *The Loss of Happiness in Market Democracies.* New Haven: Yale University Press.

McPhee, J. (1968). *The Pine Barrens.* New York: Farrar, Straus and Giroux.

Mill, J.S. (1993). *On Liberty and Utilitarianism.* New York: Bantam Books.

Nabhan, G. and Trimble, S. (1994*). The Geography of Childhood: Why Children Need Wild Places.* Boston: Beacon Press.

Neill, A.S. (1960). *Summerhill.* New York: Hart.

Noddings, N. (1984). *Caring: A Feminine Approach to Ethics and Moral Education.* Berkeley: University of California Press.

Noddings, N. (2002). *Starting at Home: Care and Social Policy.* Berkeley: University of California Press.

Rorty, A. (ed.) (1980). *Essays on Aristotle's Ethics.* Berkeley: University of California Press.

Twain, Mark (1984). *Huckleberry Finn.* New York: Library of America.

Whitman, W. (1982). *Poetry and Prose.* New York: Library of America.

Wilson, E.O. (1984). *Biophilia.* Cambridge: Harvard University Press.

Zeldin, T. (1994). *An Intimate History of Humanity.* New York: Harper Collins.

INDEX

Abrahami, Bertha, 123, 136, 145, 152

Adorno, Theodor, 25, 133

All for the Country Party, 129

Angela's Ashes, 70, 73, 82

Antonescu, Marshall Ion, 129, 135

Appelfeld, Aharon, 133, 140, 148

Ariès, Phillippe, 16, 34, 160

Aristotle, 25, 200-2, 209, 215

Arzi, Yitzhak, 139

Auschwitz, 19, 25, 133, 139, 140, 149

Auschwitz and After, 149

Baby and Child Care, 54

Bachelard, Gaston, 22, 208

Barracks, The, 80, 82, 100

Bauman, Zygmunt, 133

Beast in the Nursery, The, 28

Bend for Home, The, 83

Benjamin, Lya, 130

Bennett, William, 199

Binet, Alfred, 55

'Breaking the Cycle', 110

Browne, Noel, 91-2, 100

Bulger, Jamie, 2, 161-2

Burke, Eimear, 74

Carp, Matatias, 141

Cartea Neagra (*the Black Book*), 141

Ceausescu, Nicolae, 134

Chesterton, G.K., 71, 217

childhood,
    changing perspectives on, 1-29

Children of the Dead, 73

Children's Act, 1908, 74, 87

Children's Parliament, 2

Chomsky, Noam, 161

Christian Brothers, 86

Civilisation and Its Discontents, 26

Cosgrave, W.T., 71

'cosmopolitan family', 9, 51-68
    postmodern, 57-64
        cosmopolitan adolescent, 62-3
        cosmopolitan child, 60-2
        exchange of sexual values, 63-4
        perceptions of parents, 59-60
        roles, 58
        values, 58

Countrywoman, The, 77, 80, 82, 95, 97

Cowan, Peadar, 86

Coyle, Kathleen, 78

Crowe, Catriona, 69-70, 89

Cunningham, Hugh, 41

Dáil na nÓg, 2
Delbo, Charlotte, 149
Demos, John, 45
de Valera, Eamon, 11, 72
Devlin, Edith, 79, 82, 88
Dewey, John, 201
Dickens, Charles, 213
Dor, Orna Ben, 126
Doyle, Paddy, 76, 84, 87, 91
Dublin Society for the
    Prevention of Cruelty to
    Children (DSPCC), 74
Dunne, Seán, 78, 88, 100

Educational Research Centre,
    118
Elias, Norbert, 16
Elder, John, 209
Elkind, David, 6, 8-11, 14
Ellenbogen, Martha, 132, 136,
    137, 142, 144, 146, 147, 152
Exploring Masculinities
    programme, 114

Fahey, Bernadette, 77, 94, 96, 99
'Fear, The', xv
Ferriter, Diarmaid, 6, 11-13
Flynn, Mannix, 76, 77, 87
Freud, Sigmund, xv, 26, 27-8, 55
Frost, Robert, xv, 23, 209
Future of an Illusion, The, 28
Froude, James Anthony, 36

Gander at the Gate, 90
Garden, The, 98
Geoghean, James, 84
Gesell, Arnold, 54
Gillis, John, 6, 7-8, 14, 17
Glassberg-Gold, Ruth, 131, 138,
    142, 144, 145, 146, 148
God of Small Things, The, 165
God Squad, The, 76

Goff, Annabel, 100
Goodenough, Elizabeth, 33
Gopnik, Alison, 33, 46
Greven, Philip, 38
Gutman, Tatyana, 127

Hall, G. Stanley, 55
Harbinson, Robert, 79, 95, 97
Hard Times, 213
Haughey, Charles, 87
Head Start programme, 115
Healy, Dermot, 83, 88, 95
Heaney, Seamus, 23, 195, 209
Higonnet, Anne, 43
Hirsch, Marianne, 125, 152
Huckleberry Finn, 214
Hume, David, 211

Illiescu, President, 135
International Adult Literacy
    Survey (IALS), 116
Iron Guard, 129, 130, 142

Keneally, Thomas, 151
Kennedy, Finola, 85
Kennedy Report, 87
Kerrigan, Gene, 88-9, 93, 96-7, 99,
    101, 102
Kiberd, Declan, 70
Kierkegaard, Søren, 64
Kincaid, James, 31

Lady's Child, A, 83
Lagerwey, Mary, 139, 151
Lane, Robert, 203
Langer, Lawrence, 149, 151
Legion of the Archangel Saint
    Michael, 129
Lentin, Ronit, 6, 18-21, 25
Levy, Barry, 35
Litani, Dora, 138
Luibhéid, Colm, 99

Macnamara, John, 108
Maher, Liam, 71
Maher, Seán, 88, 102
Malaparte, Curzio, 130
McCourt, Frank, 70, 73, 80, 92,
    95, 102-3
McGahern, John, 80, 82, 93, 94-6,
    100
McGill, Patrick, 73-4
McKay, Susan, 84
McPhee, John, 210
McQuaid, Archbishop John
    Charles, 85
Miles, Clement, 43
Mill, John Stuart, 202-3
Millay, Edna St Vincent, 194
Miller, Henry, 53
Morgan, Mark, 6, 13-5
Moylan, Sean, 86

National Children's Strategy, 2,
    18
National Society for the
    Prevention of Cruelty to
    Children (NSPCC), 85
Neill, A.S., 212
Night Train to Mother, 154
Noddings, Nel, 6, 22-6
Nothing to Say, 76
nuclear family, 52, 53-7
    child perceptions, 55-6
    parent perceptions, 54-5
    perceptions of adolescents,
    56-7
    roles, 53
    values, 53

O'Brien, George, 94, 97, 102
O'Casey, Sean, 97
O'Connor, Lily, 79, 92
O'Connor, Rory, 90-1

O'Duffy, Eoin, 84
Ofer, Dalia, 126
O'Faoláin, Nuala, 78, 82, 102
Ombudsman for Children, 2
Ostfeld, Klara, 137-8
O'Sullivan, Eoin, 75
O'Sullivan, Maurice, 83, 89
'Our Children, Their Lives', 2

Palti, Sonia, 136
Parsons, Tallcott, 53
Philips, Adam, 28
Plato, 26
Postman, Neil, 16, 162-4, 166
'postmemory', 19, 125, 152-4
'Prelude, The', xiv
Primary Curriculum Review
    Body, 109

Raftery, Mary, 75
Relationships and Sexuality
    Programme (RSE), 109, 112
Revised Curriculum, 108-9
Rilke, Rainier Maria, 23, 209
Robinson, Mary, 87
Robson, Catherine, 42, 43
Roy, Arundhati, 165

Safran, Alexadre, 135
Sattinger, Rebecca, 153-4
Schindler's Ark, 151
Schindler's List, 151
Semel, Nava, 124, 126, 150
Shatter, Alan, 87
Sheridan, Peter, 77, 81, 92
Simpsons, The, 59
Simyonovich, Mark, 136
Smith, Paul, 77, 80, 82, 95
Smyth, Marie, 6, 15-8
Social, Personal and Health
    Education programme (SPHE),
    119

Sontag, Susan, 44
Sophia's Story, 84
Spock, Benjamin, 54
Starkie, Enid, 82
Stay Safe programme, 109, 114
Steedman, Carolyn, 34
Steigman-Carmelly, Felicia, 134, 137, 142, 147
Stone, Lawrence, 35
Strong, L.A.G., 91, 97
Subjective Well-Being (SWB), xv, 22, 202-3, 216
Substance Misuse Prevention Programme, 109
Suffer the Little Children, 75, 76, 88

Taylor, Alice, 89-90
To School through the Fields, 89
Touher, Patrick, 94
Transnistria, the Hell, 136
Tropic of Cancer, The, 53, 58
Tuairim Report, 1966, 87

Twain, Mark, 214
Twenty Years a Growing, 83, 89

United Nations Convention on the Rights of the Child, 2, 160

Vershoyle, Moira, 98
Village of Longing, The, 94
'virtual child', 7, 31-49
Volovici, Loen, 150

'Walk Tall' programme, *see* Substance Misuse Prevention Programme
Warner, Marina, 33, 46
Whitman, Walt, 23, 208-9, 215
Winnicott, Donal, 54
Wordsworth, William, xiv-xvi, 40

Zeldin, Theodore, 206
Zion, Shmuel Ben, 136
Zuckermann, Rosa Ruth, 145